AFRICAN MEDITATIONS

AFRICAN
MEDITATIONS

FELWINE SARR

Translated by Drew S. Burk
Foreword by Souleymane Bachir Diagne

A UNIVOCAL BOOK

UNIVERSITY OF MINNESOTA PRESS
MINNEAPOLIS
LONDON

Published by the University of Minnesota Press
111 Third Avenue South, Suite 290
Minneapolis, MN 55401-2520
http://www.upress.umn.edu

ISBN 978-1-5179-1389-2 (pb)

A Cataloging-in-Publication record for this book is available from the Library of Congress.

Printed in the United States of America on acid-free paper

The University of Minnesota is an equal-opportunity educator and employer.

31 30 29 28 27 26 25 24 23 22   10 9 8 7 6 5 4 3 2 1

CONTENTS

FOREWORD

Souleymane Bachir Diagne

Nietzsche draws our attention to this initial truth that a thought appears to us when it wants to and not when we want it to. And it's for this reason that we shouldn't say "I think" but, at best, "it thinks." And even "it" says a lot! Sometimes certain thoughts arrive that require our care and that we must know how to welcome, to grant them a body; we must know how to caress them, allow them to flow between our fingers, so as to look at them from various angles and gently forge their shape by way of a musical hammer so as to truly discern their emanating fragrance and just what illumination and sound they furnish us with: one must know how to experience these thoughts in every sense of the word. Effectuating these different operations and practices is called "to meditate." And to meditate is what Felwine Sarr invites us to do with him.

Such thoughts can be the fermata of the most banal of experiences, interrupting the laziest of reveries. A case in point: the narrator is in Saint-Louis-du-Senegal reading a book on a terrace with a view of the river; he spots a pile of trash sitting in the road that shouldn't be there, indicating poverty, filth; this whimsical carelessness takes hold of his gaze, and then, suddenly, the following thought that "from anywhere on this great earth, we can raise our gaze up to the heavens." The remark stops there but it continues to work on us as readers. For instance, it can lead to a reflection on Job sitting on his own pile of manure: when everything is reduced to nothing, the spirit—that is to say, the force of belief—still raises its gaze to the heavens and skies above.

The thoughts or meditations offered in the following pages are therefore sometimes born out of narrations. Some are dated and speak of conversations or activities held with people that are somewhat well-known—we see, for instance, an encounter with a writer friend, Louis Camara; colleagues from the university; we see mention of the former Senegalese president Abdoulaye Wade, who calls for tidying up certain streets in Dakar and clearing off the nomadic merchants who sell their wares there, in order for nothing to trouble the "summit" of his OCI . . . We could therefore say that these pages are taken from the author's own journal. There are reasons to believe that this is the case, and, as with any journal, that these pages are autobiographical fragments, often interrupted, but whose thread runs from one meditation to another.

If by "journal," one means the genre to which the Stoic emperor Marcus Aurelius jotted down his letters of nobility in writing *Pensées pour moi-même,* then, yes: this is a journal. Like this César philosopher, Felwine Sarr offers us thoughts that are "for himself" and therefore for anyone for "whom that which is human is foreign." These fragments bear no strict form, often presented as narration, sometimes as a rapid character sketch (what Felwine calls an "archetype," which he partakes in with the casuistic humor of a La Bruyère). Most often they take the form of an aphorism: a concentrated form of signification that asks the reader to pause and reflect, to recite the phrases back to themselves (sometimes these lines even take on the veritable promise of a poem), to slowly open these flowers of thought and, along with them, their petals replete with meaning. To have the phrases turn over again and again in one's head. In other words: to ruminate over them. Here again, we can turn to Nietzsche, who teaches us that to meditate requires us first to be instructed, huddled around the great cows of this supreme art of rumination.

In contrast then to Descartes's *Meditations,* the following meditations are to be read so as to remind us that thought is not the product of some disincarnated spirit at rest but is rather a practice and activity of a body in movement. "Meditate in action," Felwine Sarr rightly tells us, and we would be wise to listen to this master of composing the spiritual body with those arts we refer to as the martial arts. We should recall that comparisons between thinking and dancing have been made by Nietzsche but also by Léopold Sédar Senghor. And here the reader will also partake in the omnipresence of music, all kinds of music, with which these *African Meditations* ruminate in rhythm.

AFRICAN MEDITATIONS

An explosion reverberating throughout the entire Universe, everywhere, simultaneously, spreading throughout all space. Nothing but heat. An unimaginable warmth: 100 billion degrees centigrade. So warm that no particle of matter whatsoever can maintain its cohesion. Elementary particles spew out in all directions. A total irruption of time and space. Initial vibrations, secondary vibrations. Attractions, collisions, repulsions, pairings, then slowly, through an agglomeration of wandering astral material, the planets are formed.

～

Several billion years later, we have Lake Chad. An immensity and poetry of place, empty and vacuous. Mirroring of the first skies and the clearest of waters. An initial flourishing, frail movements, beginnings, tensions, profound undulatory movements, primordial bubblings, emergent desires, the germs of organic life, emergence. A hummingbird flaps its wings, takes flight, and perches itself on the branch of a fig tree.

～

A hummingbird feels this initial vibration and reproduces it in turn by beating its wings. Toumaï emerges from out of this initial tumulus, raises his arms up and folds them: resonant of the rhythm of the Universe. Human life hatches. Its very pulse beats within this intermediary zone between twilight and night.

~

Toumaï promptly rises from out of his bed, he hadn't heard the first beeps from the alarm clock. He only has about thirty minutes to still make it to work on time. He doesn't like having to rush in the mornings. No time to take a quick shower, enjoy a cup of coffee, nor meditate on a couple of lines from the Shobogenzo. On the way, he thinks about his family. His kids are probably already taking notes at school. Minta has probably already negotiated with her mother about what clothes she'd like to wear; "her tastes in clothes are a bit too revealing for a girl her age and her demeanor, a bit too stubborn as well," he thinks to himself.

~

Mi hé réta.[1] Such words reverberated like a thunderbolt inside the heart of Khady. She had dreaded them for so long, but from out the depths of her soul, she'd rather hear such words than nothing at all, nothing but an eternal silence of a quick departure that she knew to be unavoidable. A pain-laden sky all her own had begun to construct itself on those days when the first boys on the island had successfully reached the Spanish coastline safe and sound. And several months later, they would flood their girlfriends back home with text messages, using up their small amount of cellphone minutes. It was now Mame Khady's second attempt at fleeing the country. The first time, the pirogue had left him on the island. It had taken some time for him to collect his belongings back. His mother, Khady, having felt something of a coup was coming, had hidden them. And though his friends waited for him on the beach, as Mame Khady finally reached the shoreline, he could see the boat out on the distant horizon and that they had already left without him, before the high tide returned. Khady could hear a long whimpering breath, sobbing, shaking the tiny but solid house, then there was nothing but a heavy silence that loomed over the house for weeks. Mame Khady wandered through the home screaming like a zombie. There was a shimmer in his eyes like those who had already left the country. And Khady, Mame Khady's mother, replied: "May God take care of you, my child, and provide you shelter whereby no evil will harm you, depart in peace."

~

The cries of thought and the stammering of art must clothe themselves with pudor and await their ripening in the shadows outside the gaze of others. This is only so as to render the proper respect to the intellectual and artistic masterpieces of humanity, products of an entire millennium. A beautiful work that has attained a certain maturity can certainly then offer itself up in the light of day to nourish humankind. To provide a proper nectar, to help grow and allow them to gain in the élan or force of their ascension. Friedrich descended from Sils Maria, Sédar offered his black communion wafers, Saint Simon hid his manuscripts, but his words, through their very force, nevertheless still found their way to be consumed by humanity. Ripe fruit falls from the trees. Sometimes it leads to the happiness of both men and beasts, sometimes it merely ripens and falls to the ground and rots under the shade of trees and returns to the earth so as to nourish life itself.

~

The July light permeated the entire abode. The tiniest particles of dust, stunned by their own intimacy, emigrated to the
darkest corners of the dwelling. Two consciousnesses, face to
face. Silence no longer was capable of containing the truth of
their being. Such being should burst forth, but words couldn't
bear this weight. It was all too cumbersome for them. The
house had become the site of an impossible encounter for all
of them. Toumaï could feel it in his bones that what he was
feeling no ear was prepared to hear. Society didn't provide
spaces for such words to be expressed in the light of day. Society merely provided a place for those words that continued
to maintain its foundations and help it uphold the status quo.
Silence merely authorized resentment and bad faith. He allowed himself to simply not hear what he was saying. At bottom, he thought, nobody had ever really understood another.
Most of the time, in the best of cases, a successful relationship
was nothing more than a well-managed misunderstanding.
Over time, he had simply forgone long, drawn-out explana-
tions and rejected confiding to words what the existence of
the other could include. We were rarely accustomed to opening ourselves up and fully embracing reality in all its nudity.
Truth is also an affair of weight and structure. His was woven
with a somber and clear mixture of threads, irreconcilable
propositions and assumed paradoxes. It contained neither
the clarity of flowing rivers or lakes, nor the trenchant acuity
of a Hausa blade. It was a dwelling composed of rocky foundations and a complex architecture. For too long we had pre-
tended that the truth was singular, that it was a harmony, that
it followed a straight path like the ridgeline of a mountain.
But his truth comprised moreso a complex of islands that no
bridge connected. Knowing how to retain all of them within

their singular asperities, assuming their contradictions, such was the dimension he had taken upon himself to learn to open himself up to. The invigorating source that irrigated their relation had been obstructed for some time now. The élan toward the other had become blocked. Embrace everything? It goes without saying that this required a great amount of wisdom, but how could one continue to live within a place that obstructed the very source of life within his utmost being?

FRIDAY, OCTOBER 3

We finally arrived at Saint-Louis at 11:30 AM to light rainfall. At l'Île nord, on the rue Blanchot to a black gate, a veranda, some bougainvillea, and to a vast assortment of luminescent open spaces. The children spread themselves out, running about to discover the new spatial contours of their life: they are happy. I can sense L.—for the moment, half-serious, half-lighthearted—perhaps this is the recognition of the perspective for soon having to expand the horizons that mitigate these sentiments.

～

When the call of the muezzin can be heard resonating, it's not God that calls us forth; it's a man's voice calling you to prayer. It's the tradition, the ritual that is reassuring, the community that convokes at fixed hours is not our élan toward infinity but rather the very proof of God's existence. In offering life, God also in the same moment granted us his own existence in every instant and in every place.

～

When the joy that accompanies love only makes itself heard in brief intermittent moments, and all that remains is remorse, guilt, and the fear of breaking from one's habits, it is time to raise oneself up and immigrate to another region in this vast territory that is Love.

~

Power outages, water shortages, long lines at the bank, slow Wi-Fi connections, and so on. All these inconveniences and annoyances were symptoms of a lack of infrastructural development or, for some, signs of deficient social organization. Such "annoyances" induce a nonneurotic relation to commodities; one rediscovers their meaning and takes to renewing their utility. The patience that these "inconveniences" impose on us, us moderns, also invites us to reflect and constantly *revisit* the notion of necessity. The forecasting and cautious frugality in which we have become accustomed to these water shortages serves as a remedy against the wasting of such a vital resource in these maddening times.

~

We can inhabit the site of these capitulations and bask in their warmth. Within this *habitus*, the cold, dry wind of a guerrilla struggling against itself can no longer be felt. Nor the sentiment of a pearl of sweat still dripping from the effort of such self-overcoming. To refuse the extensive heat of such a shelter in exchange for a hole-laden tent allowing for a breeze to pass through and whereby one can catch a glimpse of the sky.

~

There are certain dénouements for which no solutions exist, where one discovers that no entirely acceptable resolution is possible. As such we are destined to kill life in order to live, to prune ourselves in order to fly, such is the implacable law of life, the cruel lot of our species. A difficult mourning for one's loss of innocence. A difficult acceptance of necessity.

~

When someone takes to begrudgingly handing over their life to you, projecting onto you psychological needs that are rooted in a complex history of their own specific origins, of their childhood, and their specific obsessional neuroses, and those that have been transmitted to them by way of their very own milieu; when, taken to madness, in refusing to accept reality outside of their own personal desires and asks you to take to sculpting out of the world some sort of dream house; and you yourself, as a tributary of your own history and your own élan, can neither properly respond to this request that falsely bears the name of love, and yet, in spite of everything, you still hold in esteem the person in question, but can only grant some sort of nonreception of their expectations of you, one certainly experiences a certain pain. Here, pain and refusal are both necessary: a true relation to things requires such a response.

~

There is something inevitable about the growth of a fig tree: it must always penetrate its way through the dark shade of previous foliage and creeping vines. It will cut a path through walls of cement and marble slabs. Nothing can stop its ascension, its vital need for air and light.

~

Since time is imperfect, one must make the best possible use of it, to extract its finest sap, acquire its best grains for sowing the future crops of humanity.

~

Proximity can become terrifying when it no longer allows one to inhale a breath of fresh air. When, in spite of one's own photosynthesis, one is no longer able to exhale a breath that can serve in turn to grant a vital breath to another. When such a proximity no longer allows one to deploy one's own being nor receive shelter from the powerful wind gust that stunts its growth.

~

A safe distance is required for all things. A space for the circulation of winds, for rejuvenating breaths. A decontaminating space. An average distance between. Space must adjust itself for those who love their neighbors without indulgence, in spite of themselves, in spite of any temptation to generalize the abyss or to collectivize fear. There is no public or private work built at the center of a generalized promiscuity. Those who truly love their neighbors sometimes must separate themselves, granting themselves a bit of elbow room, to allow for a bit of humanity.

~

Some individuals require the force of chaos in their lives. Therefore, they create destructive tornados and tempests, becoming intoxicated by such turbulent winds to momentarily escape their distress.

MAXIM FOR A RAINY DAY

Second hexagram: yin. Earth, mother, the feminine. Yin is that which welcomes, absorbs, accepts, and offers up her breast to everyone, in all circumstances. Increasing the capacity for absorption.

Intransigence: the tensing of muscles—to set off climbing up the mountain once again.

Monolith, hermetically sealed, without fissures or cracks.

To renew the conversation with those who crystalize, to attach oneself to the margins.

An explosive parsimony.

~

Everything has been graciously given to me. Concomitantly. Pains and remedies, poisons and antidotes, tests accompanied by correlative growth, times of difficult sowing and radiant flourishing. So I cannot complain.

~

Quignard wrote: "Life between men and women is a perpetual storm. The air between their faces is more intense—more hostile, all the more fulgurant—than that between trees and stones. Sometimes, on rare occasions, beautiful occasions, lightning truly strikes, and really kills. That's love."

~

We are guilty of the simple activity of not letting light pass through us. To barricade its entry by way of our somber bodies, of not carving out rows for it to pass through us and to truly be absorbed and not merely refracted by the shadows. Guilty of not being good conductors of this light.

We are guilty of diverging from light's trajectory, of attenuating its brilliance, of depriving its warmth from all its addressees.

We are guilty of not responding to a smile, and instead grumble rather than offer up a brief hello, guilty of not welcoming the day ahead via a lacerating humor, of not welcoming it with the lightest of hearts found within the flapping wings of hummingbirds and the subsequent rays of sunlight that travel millions of miles each daybreak to reach their destination so the day can begin anew.

And in so doing, we're already preparing ourselves again for night.

～

My friend Alexandre has created a magnificent place called *Autour de la terre*. We all huddle up there when we want to flee the noise of the world for a brief moment. Filled with umbrellas, chairs, wooden tables, canapés, and a great pile of books. A patio opens onto a fountain, a shadow of leaves, and a capricious sky. Enveloped by a beautiful music, one can find the most wondrous teas and coffees from the world over. The chief of the locale, the local bodhisattva, with a mischievous gaze and a welcoming smile, knew how to make of it a haven of peace. He constructed it in such a way so as to ensure that everything didn't *function* too well. So as to ensure that those who were a bit more elitist, aggressive of spirit, or too hip didn't want to settle in there. We take our time here, we pay when we can, and we simply partake in conversation. It's the lone site in this beautiful country where people seem to speak spontaneously with each other. The matchmaker introduces soulmates, with open and closed hands, utopias and their earthly asylums. Never a word is spoken that is lower than the baritone breath of friendship. The geography of the site allows one the chance to present one's illuminated face to the other, and the master of proximity, from a distance, watches over this rigorous yet fashionable fraternity.

~

We should not become embittered or luminous in confronting the test.

Its harsh wind, ruffling through our fur and masks, giving rise to a certain pleasure from within us by way of its shaded leaves where we keep our souls hidden (our hearts). And, in one's dwelling, we finally show ourselves as we truly are. My dear immodest friend, these tests only reveal us to ourselves.

~

Hatred is fidelity to resentment. Its air heavy and putrid. Its toxicity affects the heart, head, lungs, temperament, and liver. Take leave from its toxic fumes. Flee farther, deeper. Wisdom of dried herbs in front of crackling embers.

~

A temporality: a conjunction of situations: beings and things suddenly restore me to myself. My dreams of monastic exile in search of peace have subsided. It is finally here (she reveals herself to me): peace, from now on, across this vast piece of earth where the two arms of the Senegal River wrap themselves around each other. In order to appear, she requires an (interior) disentanglement. One must construct a clearing, for our lady peace does not like confusion nor does she inhabit a pigsty. The tempo of the Île nord of Saint-Louis slows down my hastened pace, born from years of endless urgency; as the location of my arrival, it becomes the site of my motionless pilgrimages, I once again learn to partake in a slowness. The temperature is almost ideal. It leads to an endless flowering of springtime. As I wait for Naïssan, I get settled down. No! I won't wait any longer, spring is already here. A Sahelian University that lives according to the rhythms of the country: student strikes, staff strikes, professors who have disappeared from their duties for not being paid on time, union struggles to restore infrastructure that has degraded, all of this merely affords the occasion to take some time for myself. I can practice the Shotokan path, remain seated in Zazen without a goal nor a mind focused on profit. Run in the mornings, read in the evenings, play music, write during the day, take care of educating Gnilane and Fahkane and serve as an example to preach at my brother, Youssou: stay in angulo.

~

The ancients referred to the discipline I teach at the university as oikonomia. It bears its name rather well, it's my discipline. I hold to it with a consistency and fidelity. Sometimes I even procure a bit of happiness from this exercise. Perhaps it's fairly useful to serve as a teacher for how to manage rarity: to allocate resources in an optimal manner and so on. The spirit for flight requires a certain amount of tarmac (be it smooth or rough) to ensure the body has its essential needs for the horizon of life to not merely be reduced to a bowl. Long years of practicing the path, wandering, have taught me the virtues of discipline, of self-discipline (and the latter can sometimes be rather supple). One can't (nor shouldn't) always be guided by one's inclinations. A tree's growth is supported by the consistency of its trunk, the spurting forth of a torrent by the stability of a rock. We are not always useful only where we feel at home, for this would be to reduce our potentialities to our tastes or preferences; truly opening one's arms out wide is what allows for any (self) discipline.

~

A promise is an attempt to freeze time, the flow of life, and its currents . . .

A promise likes to reduce the infinite potentialities of life into one (lone) occurrence. Every promise is a lie, even when fulfilled.

~

All of this reveals what I already know, but which I had already refused to fully stare down, hoping that I was mistaken, not wanting to trust my own senses, or believing that time alone would induce change, a metamorphosis . . . So I sat down in front of a nice canvas gifted to the gaze of an adolescent who refused to see reality clearly, in all its utter nudity. I've finally stopped being offended by all of this. I've stopped wanting things or beings to be anything other than what they are at the moment when they are.

~

An interior court with high walls. The path of the Shotokan can be practiced there with complete discretion.

~

I've finally understood that my life was here. Under the rays of sunshine filtered through the leaves of a frangipane tree. The weather under this sun was more fantastic. It allowed me to feel a sense of its burning force. An existence made of giving up myself, without calculations, without warning, suited me fine. Choose the tent under which one awaits the arrival of evening, the friends with whom one chats about finitude, the sites where we grant ourselves a bit of distance from the educational asylum to partake in beauty; the inner courtyard within which we refine the quality and intensity of the vibration that binds us to the pulse of the cosmos, the station where we cultivate our compassional proximity to all beings, the space wherein one sets into rhythms the cadence of our smiles and the salt of our tears. In the end, that's what choosing one's life was all about. The zero point of wandering. Establishing oneself, carving out one's path, digging deep into the earth like a worm. To finely discern the abyss. To discern the heavens.

~

Discerning the abyss. Recognizing that this vast opening will never remain full for long. Having attained a certain fullness again, the cup will quickly empty itself. Condemned as we are to wander toward the other, we are equally condemned to remain impoverished.

NOVEMBER 28, 2008

Yesterday I went to Nidarème for the funeral of my friend Bassa Sylla's father. Mahawa Sylla, a former military policeman, who had organized his life like a musical score, including the very final moments whose aspects he had already laid out. He had even gone to leaving the exact amount of money necessary for paying for his funeral arrangements, detailing every last cost for the services and preparations with a military rigor (including the menu for the dinner afterward). And in so doing, he allowed for his family to avoid having to deal with all the logistical madness that often is an additional part of mourning, making it even more difficult. Throughout his entire life, he had remained steadfast to the consistency of the tonality that he had bestowed upon himself. His family who mentioned that this monsieur who never wanted to bother anyone, and who discretely helped a lot of people around him, had always carefully arranged and limited his daily meals, his consumption of electricity, and his water usage, which he never exceeded. In this way, he had known how to avoid a great number of bad habits and ordeals inherent to Senegalese society: waste, expenses on prestige, exhausting and sterile social events, baptisms, and grandiloquent weddings . . . His widow and his children, bearing witness to their spouse and father, were able to retain a great serenity. The life lessons he left to them were immense: composed of courage, correctness, bounty, and consistency. I knew his children; his wisdom had rubbed off on them. The oldest daughter of the family, P. Sylla, who was by his side during the last weeks of his life, recounted peacefully with a tenderness (and sometimes with humor) a number of anecdotes that helped connect all these instants together for the exiled sons, who quickly returned home, as soon as they learned the news of his passing. A happy and welcoming atmosphere resonated in contrast to the sad spectacle that often accompanies most families (as much here as elsewhere) in such circumstances, during such days of mourning (or rather days of remembering). The behavior of his family displayed just how profound the roots were of the tree planted by Mahawa Sylla, whose fruits and shadow served as both a refreshing tonic and granted a welcome shade. So it was that I had the most profound and fruitful encounter with this honored monsieur, only several days after his death. Senegalese society is reputed for the forces of its social obligations. Here was a man who led and steered his boat against the winds and tides. He succeeded in being, having, and doing what he wanted to be, have, and make of his life. Such was the definition that the ancient Greeks gave to happiness. From out of all this, I retain a certain conviction that the course of one's life is a force against which the world can do nothing. Such a disposition is necessary for a happy life.

~

The roads in this country are where one prays the most. Do you want to feel alive? Take off on one of these roads! Every last driver runs red lights! The one who drives you, with his fellow automobilists surrounding him, the donkeys, the cows, the horse-drawn carts, the goats, the chaos, and the undisciplined nature of it all, along with the maddening stupidity of the fatalism of the pedestrians, and there you have it. An overwhelming sentiment of despair and powerlessness and a quasi-absence of the recognition of the level of risk that one takes. Within this minefield, the least disastrous option is to mount one's own chariot and drive oneself, slalom out in a straight line, priding oneself only in one's talent for paving the way for the Grim Reaper.

~

My personal god: my aspiration toward truth in every act, in every thought, in every sentiment.

~

Every morning, the call.

~

Escaping the solidified self. Liquidating it, vaporizing it, dispersing it out over a thousand winds.

~

A man walks towards me with a resolute step. He waves for me to stop. We go through the usual greetings. He doesn't know me. He's an adjunct lecturer, he says. He has spent the day on campus hoping to find something to feed his family. The month has been pretty rough and he hasn't been paid yet. On the road farther along, I ask myself: would I have done the same thing in his place? Certainly not! But, in the end, I realize that *dignity* is a superfluous clothing when one lacks the essential things, the bare minimum for survival. Was not the first of dignities the ability to feed oneself? Is it a pitiful act to ask of the other, "Help me to drink from the source of life"? This morning, the same individual tried to stop me again. I was in the car this time and I didn't stop. At the end of the day, upon leaving, I relented and listened to his story, and just as quickly I was embarking onto his entire history, with one lone alternative: to partake in solidarity or not. Speech, hearing, language, engages and connects. To speak, listen, and respond to a gaze is already to partake in solidarity.

～

Sunday morning. A free day. Words are waiting at the train station, waiting to depart. The feelings they want to express are already present, raw but obscure. The seduction of the blank page and the ruse of a text that expresses their absence fails to entice them to arrive. To inhabit a pure nonmediated presence, such is our lesson for today.

～

The Corniche. On the left bank of the island far beyond the Faidherbe bridge. A seawall extends the path along the river. A new neighborhood is slowly but surely under construction. Piles of rubbish are still there, polluting the environs of the river. At the end of a long chaotic path of laterite avoided by the taxis, one can see a great red ochre building. Here we find Khabane living with his wife, Soukaina, and their children. He tells me that he was the first person to settle here. Everyone thought he was mad. We make our way up to the living quarters, and I sit down at the terrace with a book in my hand, taking in an incredible panorama. Directly in front of me lies the great majesty of the Senegal River; to my left, piles of trash sit alongside where children are playing. At 4:15 in the afternoon in this corner of the world, a rather sober sun radiates across the horizon, calming the waters. Khabane and Fahkane are in the adjacent room. With care, patience, ardor, and exigency, the master transmits to the disciple the secrets of the exercise that untangles fingers and the musical notes that pierce souls. One can hear airs of Beethoven echoing out from this site on the path: first a cheerful, steady melody (the maestro is playing), then a somewhat shaky and unsure series of attempts (the student is trying their hand at the piece). In surveying, to my left, the piles of rubbish that linger, I think to myself, and there is no doubt: from anywhere on this great earth, we can raise our gaze up to the heavens.

～

Two months ago, only a couple of days had passed upon my arrival to this island when I heard whispers of a gathering around the work of Julien Gracq. They talk about Julien Gracq here!? I thought to myself. I went to the conference at the CRDS at the southernmost point of the island. In front of a rather sparse but nevertheless attentive crowd, Boubacar Camara graciously provided us with an excellent presentation on the life and work of Julien Gracq. And it was at this conference that I would meet Louis Camara, a writer from Saint-Louis who received the *prix du Président de la République for Letters* in 1996, passionate about Yoruba mythology and who, to my pleasant surprise, only lived a couple of meters away from me the next street over. Several days later, Louis Camara would end up taking me to the African Cultural Center at Diamaguène, one of the more popular neighborhoods in the city, to participate in a meeting with the writers and poets of Saint-Louis. They are preparing for the first International Book Fair to take place in this corner of the continent. My fresh eyes were struck first by the dilapidated character of this house of culture: dust and dirt, antiquated technology . . . "Despite the lack of means, they could have at least cleaned the place up a bit, and dusted . . . ," I thought to myself. The meeting was held in the room that served as the office of the library. Covered in spiderwebs and suffering dust-laden piles of books. And there, around a table, sat the philosophers, writers, and poets of Saint-Louis. Some of them had arrived on foot. Others had hitchhiked. Times were tough and yet they held strong. The debates were passionate, without concessions, sometimes rather lively. All the details of the organization had been carefully thought out and reflected upon. A long discussion ensued with regard to foresight and planning, as they considered what should be expected, and then they carried on with more reflections. After an hour, I had already forgotten the dust and dilapidated nature of the building. The room was suddenly filled with the light of these individuals who were profoundly passionate about culture, pouring their heart and soul into organizing the Book Fair. I learned that the Book Fair was funded by an NGO from the North who had obtain funding from silent backers and had left them some crumbs to organize a conference here in Saint-Louis. "Another sucker of the flows of the markets," I thought to myself. In any case, this group of artists assembled around me certainly weren't suckers. Their concerns were entirely elsewhere. I left the meeting reassured and regenerated by their faith.

~

Here the children partake in a joyous freedom of movement: they play in the street, wandering and running here and there; the watchful parental eye remains a rather loose leash. Beginning at the age of three, we start sending them to the store, we let them go to school on their own, move among the throngs of people, get accustomed to the chaos of the outside and learn to avoid traps. This makes for rather resourceful and unencumbered kids. Sometimes, such a freedom ends up being rather costly. The young next-door neighbor, Ablaye, four years old, had the custom of making the walk from Sor to the Île Nord without anybody ever worrying about him. After wandering off several times, everybody became accustomed to seeing him disappear for a while and then later reappear. He preferred to live at his father's house, with his brothers. For three days now he's been missing. In the beginning, we thought he had just wandered off, partaking in a fugue. And then, we found him lying in a sewage ditch, dead. It seems he had accidentally fallen.

~

Orléans, in the neighborhood of Venelle de l'écu Bellebat. A bit of the countryside within the heart of the city. Noise sometimes arrives somewhat muffled, filtered through a pâté of flowering houses that jealously watch over its tranquility. Fred and Pascale live in a house with a garden. The back door, appearing to have been installed upside down, always remains open. The front door as well. They are like two characters in a Francis Cabrel song, where he prays to the heavens that we should all be like them— *Comme Eux*: "nothing more than a smooth surface, than double-sided tape, nor a false bottom, nor any double dealing."[2] A friendship, a simplicity, a flawless complicity seem to tie them together. Their generosity is nothing but genuine. Never once have I detected the slightest of secondary motives within these uncalculating givers of self. Nothing but a nonaggressive consistency toward the bounty and élan of the Other. The grace of having folks like them in one's entourage helps overcome any sense of self-complacency. Their tranquil nature of simply being-there indicates ever so gently the distance that remains for one to traverse.

DECEMBER 5, 2008

This morning at 9 AM, L. finally departed toward other horizons, serene and at peace. And so another page was turned after thirteen years of light and darkness, of a difficult birth, of self and weaving a relation with the other. I'm grateful to the Orishas for this long companionship and the life lessons of these walks among two, three, and four. The Upanishads teach: "Know thyself- thyself." But we can only know ourselves through a relation to the other. She gifted me the best part of her, and I hope she has finally rid herself of all the tumults and turbulent waters within. It had been a very long time since I had seen that flickering gleam of light shine in her eyes. To love is also to depart. To put a distance between oneself and the past. To unburden oneself. A new day is on the horizon.

~

Naïssan was born on December 6. Naïssan is also the name for the first day of spring in the Syrian calendar. Aragon evokes this date in his work *Le Fou d'Elsa*, at the heart of the faubourgs of Albaicin, of Grenada the most beautiful, of Alhambra and the cowardice of Boabdil. For so long now, I've awaited you, *For so long now, I have loved you* . . . and from now on you are here. After a long decade wherein, by way of weariness, I had given myself over to unknown dreams, today I have rediscovered once again a vast and plentiful space replete with air. A knot that once was twisted and my throat that had for a long time been cut, has once again begun to warble, struggling to regain its amplitude, its ancient breath. To no longer be under the control of any other dictates, save for those that would restore the most beautiful of promises: such has been, for several months now, my calm resolution.

The house is empty. Fakhane has left for school. Youssou has taken Gnilane to my Aunt Fatou's to have her hair braided for the festival of Tabaski, and Ndèye—the woman who kindly prepares our meals—has yet to arrive. In the early morning hours, rue Blanchot, recently renamed rue André Guillabert (with a festive accompaniment of trombones and trumpets), lingers yet still in a dry and dreamy stupor. Even within the golden hour of the early morning and although no one is working, the street still hums with the hushed rumblings and fragile clamor of holidays. I sit Bassaï down at the end of the room and decide to take a shower, leaving the bathroom door half open. The Other, the one who can engender shame, is, for the moment, absent. I peacefully splash about, listening to such beautiful music. That of a rediscovered springtime. And one that we have resolutely decided no longer to leave.

After having always walked in a group for such a long time, the one thing I learned was that my steps were never more certain and assured (with an open hand) than when I walked alone, in the middle of the peaceful light made by Naïssan's beautiful paths.

~

My paradise is a half-open French door that gives way to a veranda covered in the benevolent shadow of the bougainvillea; rays of sunlight streaming and striating the arcana of a black balustrade. A time rediscovered, a social machinery that lessens its grip, the vibrant plunge of water as it spreads freely through the fish nets. I flip through the work of Prajnanpad, *The Banquet*, making an attempt at reading; it's not really happening. My mind and spirit are just not into it today. So, I accept and embrace this state and set the books down. I will no longer advance toward wisdom, peace, joy, or whatever else, like a madman. I begin to strum Django Reinhardt's *Accords Parfaits* and suddenly my soul starts to dance the *sama*. A progressive integration of various layers of the psyche. The gathering together of the various airs of the brain and the cells of the body into one beating heart. A cool and calm preparation for tonight's concert: the composition of the set, checking on the guitar strings to see whether I need to swap one out, I pull together some blank mini-discs to record everything . . . A profound interior calm and a self-forgetting arises in order for the music to flow from a source much more distant than oneself. The practice and repetition of music is nothing but a long preparation at transparency. The body, one's vocal chords, one's breath, along with the instruments, all must be prepared and ready in order for the transmission of primordial energy to flow so as to ensure the least loss of such energy during the transfer that radiates throughout one's being. Today, I finally baptize 238 rue Blanchot, *daraay samadhi* (the school of awakening, the school of enlightenment).

~

Once I have ventured out of it, I can no longer reenter the narrow box that comprises a culture and its certitudes.

~

The lack of means obliges one to do a lot with very little. And it's in such instances that one's talents and qualities of being, one's dormant abilities and grounded virtues, suddenly reveal themselves. Abundance momentarily leads to carelessness, to dispersion; to errors, lack, and profound fissures along with their subsequent nefarious effects; under such a coat of abundance, these flaws take more time to appear. Parsimony alone is explosive. Lest we recall the atom.

~

In the beginning, Peace (freedom) was already something that had been bestowed to us, that had been granted. Bandits and pirates perhaps then took hold of it. Henceforth, all freedom (peace) is a quest to regain it.

~

The relation to the other is the site for the quest for God and the lone site of the accomplishment of this quest. To no longer quest or seek, to fully be here, present, right here and now, is a way perhaps of avoiding fairly long detours.

~

At the heart of prayer, desire becomes vanquished, and demand collapses and crumbles. And in this manner, the last veil falls that obstructed communion with the whole.

~

The time prior to time. A paradoxical formula.

~

The matter of which we are composed only represents the tiniest part of the elements constituting the Universe. It seems to me that our absence will have not changed much at all in the greater scheme of things, in the long march of the cosmos . . .

Perhaps the Universe would have therefore lost an awakened consciousness?

~

God, in humility, has created the world such that we can explain it without him.

~

Offer up to the mortals a journey that is more stable and more durable than themselves: such is the task of an oeuvre.

~

Like the Universe, after having been hot, we too will become cold again throughout the course of time. It took much time for light to escape from the primordial abyss in order to reach us: 380,000 years of darkness. In spite of this long journey, light only illuminates 0.5 percent of the mass of the Universe. And it will take even more time for this same light to illuminate us from within.

~

An explosion gave birth to temporality (so it seems). Before time, before the origin, before creation: aporia. A chasm in thought and all representation, since time didn't exist prior to this instant without any prior.

~

Time: a bottomless web that flows even when nothing is going on, or a succession of events? In the absence of events that have taken place and passed, could we even speak of the past? Time: a perpetual present, duration, intensity, entanglement?

~

We are marginal beings composed of minoritarian elements of the Universe. We inhabit the ghetto of the galaxy, lost among the endless galactic star clusters of a universe whose limits we do not know. And yet, we are here, conscious of the Whole.

~

I dream of the silent peace of the snowfall on Mount Kilimanjaro, of calm mornings and motionless suns.

~

I reside at the summit of a supple mountain that sinks and springs back in place beneath my feet: Uhuru Peak. Flexing and stiffening beneath my fingers.

~

Tirelessly, toward the equinoxes, I walk.

~

The first time I encountered one gentleman I was immediately struck by his pride: he housed a spiritualized ego that he contemplated; he was a bit satisfied with himself. One could make out the signs of those who spend hours in prayer: crusted remnants of blackened ash on his forehead. Some folks even go to extremes to exaggerate it a bit, brushing up against the ground over and over in order to retain such distinctive marks of piety. He told me a tale of having renounced a brilliant career as a jet-setter within the corridors of power, throwing it all away in order to dedicate himself exclusively to God. Even his way of narrating his account and tending to his fire of vanities was fairly flamboyant. The flames of the ceremonial burn pile of his earthly desires had somehow begun to creep even into his tale. He had even stopped working, like a bird that neither sows nor harvests, confident in God for his subsistence. In this case, God had the face of a wife who struggled working several jobs to make ends meet for the family.

Something immediately rang false in the portrait of this humble, pious, and model family: a brother had suddenly made his entrance and just as quickly left. A shameful wound to the family: he had gone against the family's discipline, refusing the values that they wanted to inculcate in him. This gentleman is an archetype, and we find his type across cultures the world over, especially under skies where pharisaism (often unaware of itself) prospers.

～

Progressively, by way of prayer, I eliminate fear.

～

I love nothing more in a person than bounty. When will I ever experience a form of tenderness for their flaws? (Perhaps, the day I have once and for all cured my own.)

～

Little by little, through prayer, I remove the prayer, in order to remain alone with presence.

~

There is no promise that can fully contain life in its plenitude. For life will inexorably overflow such boundaries.

~

Often it begins with a subtle murmur. A confused, obscure inner voice suddenly begins to desire crafting language within an embryo of onomatopoeia. A door slightly pushed creates an opening, revolves and swivels, gasping once again. A balm soothes and melts as a scar once again becomes a scab.

~

Sacred texts don't exhaust revelation. Bogged down, solidified, altered, deviated, perverted, they end up carving out other paths. Among the work of certain artists and poets, writers and visionaries, such revelation continues to flow.

~

This morning, I wanted to visit *La lumière du monde* by Bobin and Krishnamurti's *Le livre de la meditation et de la vie*. I was prepared to go scour through a stack of books on the floor when just as quickly as I turned my head, both volumes caught my gaze, one on top of the other, sitting on a pile of books, staring back at me with a smile at the corner of their mouths as if to say, "we've been waiting for you and you finally showed up . . . well, well . . . it's not too early after all!"

~

Knowing how to wait for the nourishing moment of an encounter.

~

Call to the muezzin: a social cadence of religiosity. Call of the soul, a rhythm proper to gathering oneself, a chosen meditative time: a moment that originates within oneself.

~

Love is something one learns about only through its absence.

~

Wed oneself to lack, which alone irrigates love.

~

My Senegalese brothers have a really sturdy ego. This makes them feared competitors. When young, when their footing is still fragile, fearing the ground might be pulled out from under them, they learn to construct an edifice of stones to protect them from the wind and rain. Affirm oneself in order to exist: that's the rule. To overcome the anguish of inconsistency, they shore up their tone and steps, carefully sculpting and sharpening the blade of their desires. To undertake such a task, they must build a fire from an all-encompassing pile of wood: genealogies, heritages, forces, and pride are convoked.

At puberty such tasks can be understood. These strategies are necessary for survival, first for growth: to vanquish the perils of nature, to overcome the mineral and vegetal world, to raise one's head high above the heads and ears of millet.

Alas, the world remains within this first age. The *ego* of the world: its technological prowess, its nuclear power . . .

But later on, to take flight into the second age, it will be necessary to undo this fortress to open up the corridors of air, to throw down one's armor and dispose of all the weapons of war, and only a true force or power can do this. Even though the Tibetans were once great warriors, they eventually renounced war to attain a higher dimension of their being: awareness. Awake.

~

A grumpy mood, lukewarm, pale, bitter feelings, and rancor are sometime nothing more than retained water that needs to be evacuated. Set out on a run. Open up one's pores, sweat, and evacuate this excess plenitude of urea, and, as if by magic, everything sorts itself out. No need for sutras or mantras for that.

~

Running at dusk toward the north, toward the south, slicing through the winds, is also a path of enlightenment.

~

The absolute cannot be expressed in language. The latter can only get close to it. Every language, however beautiful it may be, is deficient, lacunary, finite. The encounter with the absolute is synonymous with the abrupt ending of a discussion. To decree or enumerate a quality of the absolute is to limit it.

~

Chapter "The Moon": Litanies of threats against the forgetful man. Reminders of the punishments inflicted for the negligence of ancient peoples. A torrential rain against the people of Noah, a violent and glacial windstorm against the Adites, the cries against the Thamüd, the hurricane against the people of Lot, except for his family saved at dawn for their good deeds. At the beginning, it's always a question of humanity treating every revelation as a lie, only following their own compulsions. That is, if they bear witness to a prodigal son turned against them, they merely tell themselves that this is only some sort of manifested magic, that any sort of warning can't possibly be useful, that the End is nigh.

"On these days, with their eyes lowered to the ground, the naysayers will rise from their tombs like fleeing grasshoppers, running with their heads held up directly toward the caller." "We will dredge the negligent into the fire by their faces and tell them: 'taste [. . .] the fiery heat of hell.'"

Such threats are made toward man so that he will become afraid and avoid evil. We would have liked for such tactics to have ceased for a time. To have moved on from the childhood of human consciousness, where the threat of club or stick to the skull was necessary for humankind to act well; in hopes that the fear of punishment would no longer be the engine of proper and good actions. As Denis Vasse put it: the law no longer had to be the mediator between yes and no, it could finally stop being the definitive and global expression of humankind and that it refers back to the inexpressible truth of being, that the letter of the law in no way alleviates man from the perpetual questioning of his actions.

"The pious will be in the gardens, among the reeds and thickets, in a journey for truth, hovering around an omnipotent lord."

Fortunately, the next chapter is that of "Misericord": a consolation for the frightened? But in the end, whoever grants me with their misericord will have already made me bow under the burden and weight of a certain fault and guilt.

~

Concerning the question of man, only man can respond.

~

Any definitive answer as concerns man is totalitarian.

~

This body that I clothe, nourish, sculpt, care for and caress, will return to the earth. It will become food for the termites. It's for this reason that I clothe, nourish, sculpt, and care for it.

~

No one knows when their final hour will arrive (except for a small few). That's what makes the adventure (the voyage) unique, singular, and determinant in each moment.

The same can be said about constructing a dwelling, and one is no longer sure if one will be capable of ever completing and living in it, such that each stone placed into the dwelling becomes its own end, the very activity of construction its own goal (its own justification).

~

The death of someone close to us opens up a wound in our sensibility. The fundamental fragility of things reappears to us. The essential vibration and trembling of life becomes at once all the more vibrant. This sudden state of immense receptivity becomes an exhaustible resource for learning.

Alas, little by little, the daily grind dulls this refined

sensitivity to beings and things, it closes up this rift that momentarily had widened our vision.

~

The heart is superior to litany.

~

When God comes toward us, he doesn't descend from the heavens on a winged horse. It's through simple and banal things. An impromptu encounter, a father who braids the hair of his daughter, Gnilane, who plays throughout the entirety of Boussoura, a sudden breeze in the midst of heatwave . . . God manifests through multiple avatars of relations to beings and things.

~

A vast wave, absolute, on a changing sea.

~

What is my practice? That of a unity with the whole. The unity of the body, of the mind and soul with the cosmos out from which they arose. An accord with the course of things. Identity with the supreme Self. A total Union of humanity with the cosmos of which it is the living eye: a contemplative conscious. The fusion of the human being (the being through which the Universe contemplates itself) with the Whole, with the Reality, which is one. Some call it Fana, others the Tao, others Maha Yoga, and yet others still, at the extreme point of this practice, refuse even to name this path since naming is already a way of separation; for those who seek unity, this naming would be a way of slowing the progression of the rays of light that lead to the center. Those who travel on a variety of rays toward the center are more closely tied together among themselves than those still on the periphery (the circumference of the circle), debating external forms, becoming divided, turning round and round instead of taking the plunge, since those who want to know the nature of water don't stay on the dock.

When such a practice seeks authenticity, it transcends forms and above all no longer conceives of itself at the center of gregariousness.

~

Humanity is my culture; Reality, the one and only universal, is my faith, better still: evidence that often takes some time to truly encounter.

~

First, obstinately dig deep into an area of ground to seek out water. Once the source has been discovered: toss the bucket aside, then plunge right in; don't swim, just drown yourself in it.

~

Only teach that which has been profoundly realized. In such moments as these, things become detached, transmigrated, and by way of some sort of impression, transmit themselves all by themselves. Only presence is truly a teacher.

~

This sensibility: it's Everest. No one, *really*—*no one*, is up to the task of such heights. It irredeemably condemns one to an empty, white solitude.

~

In Japanese, the term *nyoze*—"Thus it is, just so," "precisely so, equal"—is superior to *amen*: "so be it."

~

"Avec le temps" is the lone song about impermanence I know. Some folks consider "Ne me quitte pas" as the best French song ever written. The talented Jacques Brel, like Lamartine, pleads for the time of love to not end. Brel's beautiful song straps on his poetry as a refusal to accept the nature of change, appealing to his desires for a forced return of love *on burned fields that would yield more wheat than the best April*. The pathetic touch of it all reaches it heights when he pleads for the beloved to become *the shadow of his shadow, the shadow of his voice, the shadow of his dog*. The crooner, Léo Ferré, by way of a quasi-oriental, Heraclitian wisdom, accepts the course of things. Better, he simply harmonizes himself with them: "With time, as time flows, everything passes, we forget faces and voices, and when the heart no longer beats, there's no need to continue one's search, one must let things go, and that's just fine . . ."[3]

~

In 1951, Maama Saliou moved the Mbine Samba family to Boussoura. He was the first to settle down in this neighborhood of Niodior, which today is called O Diongola and which, during that period, was still a patch of fairly rough brush. A dozen years later, he left to seek his older brother Maama Lang at the Médina Sangako in order to bring him back from his excessively long exile. Maama Lang was a greatly respected and feared wrestler. For three years of matches, he never once touched the ground. Impossible to uproot, like a baobab from Yong-Yong, toward the end of his reign it was said that he walked with a Black *pagne* on his shoulder promised to anyone who could take him down to the ground. A foot injury (a spell cast by another wrestler, it would seem), that had not properly healed, led him to take up a desk job. He became a blacksmith, a forger, in spite of his Guelwar lineage. He was given the nickname Maama Lang Tafa (The Forger). Maama Back, the younger brother of Maama Saliou, would also be welcomed home from Bakalar, a tiny village on the opposite bank of the Gambia River (from which vantage point one can see Banjul). Maama Rassoul, the father of Maama Ami, was a carpenter. He would build huge pirogue boats, one of which was named Ri *Gambetta*, after the boulevard in Dakar boasting the same name, and another one called *Alzérie*. Then there was the long companionship between Maama Rassoul with Thierno Sylla, the marabout—the medicine man—residing in Fogny. The latter, after having predicted the future, was instructed to bestow on her daughter the name Animata. Maami Ami had four children that survived childbirth, the oldest, Mariama Sarr, my aunt. Her oldest son, my father, Mamadou Lamine, also known as the Doudou of Kaolack, would come after my aunt Binta. Three sons of Maami Ami would perish before the birth of my uncle Amadou, who was the last of her children. Ibrahima, Rassoul, Yahva. Fatou Ndour, the mother of Maama Ami, was cut down by lightning strike. She walked inside, sat down on her bed, unfastened the first strap of her *pagne* dress that held her baby on her back, and the lightning struck her, instantly killing her as well as her baby. Maama Abdou Karim, the brother of the baby she was carrying, was there and saw the whole thing but survived.

~

Everything is perfect or almost perfect. Time, a marine breeze, an adequate rhythm, a harmony with nature, always in the midst of being born. Children's games, the neighing of horses, the braying of donkeys, the breeze flowing through the branches of the coconut trees, the crackling made by feet walking over seashells. A couple of mosquitos want to spoil the festivities. Not really, in the end; thanks to them, fine white chiffon fabric hangs in the bedrooms.

AUGUST 12, 2009, 7:30 AM

Fahkane and I are running toward Yong-Yong, past the Wourrour's pile of seashells, the garden and the orchard. Kiyons, katas. A short race on the way back. After more than a month wrestling on Niodior every day, all day long with the kids his age, mounting the donkeys and seeking out pieces of dead wood, swimming at Kooko and Moûssa Diagne, Fahkane has become a young, steadfast Niominka.

~

Knowledge, recognition, renewing ties, recognizing one's own relatives, matching faces with names, reconstructing the threads of one's history, unearthing the missing pieces. In contrast to what I thought, I was actually born at Mbine Ndiaye and not at Boussoura. Toward dawn, my mother and

Maama Ami left Boussoura to go see the matron Maama Binta Cissé who predicted that I was going to be born as the sun rose early in the morning hours. Instead of making the trip all the way back to Boussoura, they waited at the birth home of my mother, not too far from the matron's abode.

Maama Secko, my godfather, tells me the story of the coconut trees: whom they belong to, what year and for what occasion they were planted there.

About the age when we must be strong, all the young men from Niodior are strong.

At what age do we become wise?

My friend Hubert Haddad wrote, "experience is never useful when we are confronted with an error, we are always new when faced with a mistake." For a long time, this comment had discouraged me. The desire to draw some kind of benefit from past mistakes, to be able to capitalize on the wisdom of lived experience so as to avoid making the same mistakes again, had a profound impact on me. What's the point, then, of all these passing days if we don't learn anything from them?

It would seem to me that, in the end, each experience bears its own message, its own novelty, its own lesson, its own illumination in the midday sun, like the slivers of will-o'-the-wisps above the oak trees on the path to Djilor; that the truth of one moment is always in the midst of chasing after a preceding one.

~

The return path: Shohravardi, Junayd, Avalokiteshvara have all made use of it. Mandela, in returning from his struggle for freedom, both exultant and exhausted, had to begin confronting the trivialities of day-to-day existence. The Nabi descend from Mont Hira, Gautama left behind the shadow of the Bodhi tree, Moses returned from Sinai . . .

Those who for a time have known great heights, those who descend from the Himalayas in ecstasy, from an encounter with love or beauty, those who have surfed on the mightiest of breaking waves, all know that the return is laden with pitfalls. That, as they progress onward on the ray of light, they won't be able to avoid crossing through fields of ruins and rubble, infested with rotten trunks.

~

Everything in this world (at this level of reality) is subject to the laws of thermodynamics. There is nothing that won't one day encounter with its own degradation. There is no truth that won't (one day) take to rot. From the highest and most supreme station, everything can be destroyed, to such an extent that nothing remains, not even breadcrumbs for a crow who won't pass by there, and who, within his beak, will carry with him the slightest hint of a blessed time, savoring the remaining flavors of nostalgia. The shadow of paradise often delights us to the point that we take it for prey.

We are only granted a glimpse, sometimes a glimpse so great that we think the door is open, that we find ourselves in the garden, where the flowers remain at their source. Alas, the door always remains but slightly cracked.

~

From now on, we will love each other, but without depersonalizing ourselves. We will love each other, but we will no longer expect love; too bad, we will no longer expect anything from love except love itself. Oh no! We will love each other, but we won't expect anything, since to love is the term for the path. To love hastens God's arrival.

~

Having partaken in a whiff of the fragrance of the kingdom (us, exiles), we set ourselves on the road ahead.

Since perfection is a unity without any addition, since nothing can be added to the Unsurpassable, to the Infinity of Paradise, only those who are nothing may enter (only nothing can enter into *apirideiza*). The *ego* that only knows self-addition, self-accumulation, being and persisting, cannot gain access.

~

The shadows are not merely within us, it's we who, in walking, bear them, dislocating them, propagating them. The only oeuvre that has any worth is to dissolve them; the lone true profession, *le seul métier: le mangeur des ombres*—the digester of shadows.

~

To fill in the remaining gap of incompleteness or tame it so peace is no longer a mere respite.

~

It is more than urgent for someone to lend me a hand, from one end of a chain of grace.

~

For the moment. The meditations stop here. Here, in Lausanne, far from African lands. I will carve out in ink the last period or attempt to draw it toward infinity. In any case, I'm still in the midst of a creative experiment, always and forever, crafting a verse of relational thermodynamics.

JOURNAL OF MY
HASTENED STEPS

MARCH 24, 2007. ZAZEN AT THE DOJO OF NOTRE-DAME DE LA RECOUVRANCE

Zen is coinciding with that which is. Being that which is without separation from the *ego*, from the mental. Incomplete teachings exist: concerning that which is good, that which is evil, etc. A horse must be whipped and also compensated in order to follow a marked path. Zen is a complete, radical teaching, taking you right to the edge. Where not one more step can be taken. Liberation. There where the *ego* can no longer grasp. One mustn't attempt to attain awareness with the *ego*. *Or conceive of awakening with the ego.* Take a step beyond the edge.

~

The book takes me by the hand and leads me to the point of a rendezvous with myself.

MARCH 26, 2007. LA FOI DIFFICILE, JEAN GUÉHENNO

This book fell into my lap by the most improbable circumstances or through the most profound necessity. I find within it the clearest, most pure and simple echo of my inner stirrings. Its expression solidifies them. Is it the gesture of the great instructor still hard at work within me?

"Here I am, old enough now to write for no other reason than for pleasure. For nothing or anyone else. Perhaps for myself? To see clearly. I think of those chemically doctored pieces of paper that, when children rub on their blank surface, lines and symbols, even colors, suddenly begin to appear. They rub and rub! What beast, what monster, what angel will this practice give birth to? We are its children. We scribble, we as well, on a mysterious blank sheet of paper without knowing exactly what forms and figures it will give rise to, but this figure, whatever it might be, in some ways reveals us to ourselves. And we continue, throughout our life, our scribblings, at once impatient and anguished to finally know who we are . . . to see ourselves [. . .] Only write for pleasure? Am I capable of this? And yet, where effort might fall short, perhaps nonchalance will win the day. So it goes: we go through life desiring, desperately desiring, and then one day we discover that this very tension that we imposed on ourselves only led us farther from the truth."

APRIL 1, 2007

Who is happy? Is it only the one not possessed by fear, anxiety, or desire? Most spiritual practices posit the expulsion of desire as the very key to happiness. Desire being only a form of torment, a lack of satisfaction, or a lack of fulfillment . . .

What other wisdom can one hope to acquire but to simply yield to that which allows for life to occur, to be maintained, and to perpetuate itself? After the great Big Bang, the wandering astral materials yielded to desire so as to coalesce and form the planets. At a certain epoque, man and woman had to desire each other for life to emerge. To become accomplished, to desire, humankind aspires. Will, striving, and desire are the myriad faces of the same force. What sort of wisdom is to be found within privation and self-amputation for fear of being dissatisfied? Sometimes desire can attain its object; that is, it attains its goal and thereby attains ecstasy. Not desiring anything at all is to not even want the expulsion of desire. It's merely to let things come forth without attempting to hinder them. The fruit ripens and falls, the tree dries out by the warm, sharp, howling winds of the rock-laden desert. Like a cresting wave, desire rises and falls through exhaustion or fulfillment.

What is empty wants to become full. That which is encumbered, craves vacuity.

That which is perfect no longer desires and works in peace.

It's life itself that, through us, desires itself and accomplishes itself.

APRIL 2, 2007

The real is that which is and that which is still becoming. What is becoming already is but has yet to become manifest. The real or reality is that which appears but also that which is hidden. The visible is intertwined with the invisible by way of a mysterious acausal chain. Christiane Singer speaks of *spaces of the real in waiting*. These spaces wait to be fertilized by our desire, our will, and our determination to grasp reality. As such, we are the very cocreators of the ether and reality in which we bathe.

APRIL 4, 2007

I just finished reading Christian Bobin's *Prisonnier au berceau*. A beautiful work. It was not so much a book I read as it was a source of light from which I drank. The rays of light shining forth from his work have cleared away the rusted iron bars once encasing my soul.

MAY 9 AND 10, 2007

I have started a new regimen. The alarm clock goes off at 4:30 AM. Eight hours of physical labor: stocking the shelves, preparing the orders, and everything else that goes with it. The body is subjected to a harsh test. Days such as these are like prolegomena, preparations for the special stage for the week to come. All my muscles are solicited for this work. My sore and aching muscles should prepare me for the next week's agenda at Vichy. Storms and tornados of all sorts. All one can do is stay strong. Remain within one's shelter and let things pass.

The first nights I would return home completely exhausted like a failed second pair of hands, on the rocks of the *pointe d'Almadies*. I was educated and created to transmit knowledge at the highest level, and here I am, like a docker at the Port of Dakar, carrying backbreaking loads simply to survive. And yet, beneath this heavy clothing of sweat and labor resides a layer of grace. Slowly but surely I sense some kind of personal providence. Not being able to properly prepare myself, I did not feel physically ready for the special test ahead, and yet now this work at the docks, and the other various tasks, have led me to call forth the help of all my body's muscles.

The movements I effectuate eight hours a day serve as a way to work my fists, biceps, triceps, knees, thighs, back muscles, endurance, tenacity, and an adequate rhythm. Today, in simply bearing the loads at the dock, I realize that I experience the same sensation as when I practiced the *sanbon kumité* last year. I'm obliged to wake at 4:30 AM in the morning and to be at work by 6:00. It's the hour of the special challenge. The internal clock can learn to regulate itself at the proper hour. Everything suddenly appears to serve for attaining a goal. And what exactly is the goal? Thanks to this manual labor, I have acquired a certain intelligence of the body. There are no useless gestures. Seek out the shortest path. Let the gesture complete itself without thinking too much about it. Allow oneself to be acted upon by this gesture. This gesture also simply seeks to accomplish itself. The spirit of the gesture. A fluidity installs itself. Being what one does. Being what one is while one is doing what one does. The potential for awareness resides within these moments of life, it inhabits each one of these gestures.

~

Ishin-denshin, from my totality to your totality, without duality, from my body to your body, from my soul to your soul, from my spirit to your spirit. As the legend goes, Bodhidharma will transport martial arts and zazen from India to China. The sixth patriarch of Eno will play an important role in the transmission of Chan, and then in that of Dogen in the thirteenth century in Japan. Then Deshimaru will bring forth this tradition in Europe throughout the twentieth century after Christ.

MAY 15, 2007

My god, I would have loved you beyond the mere words and forms that humans have bestowed upon you.

~

At the end of my street, a group of Black Mauritanians without proper documentation live in a building.

~

This life has been granted to us. When did we lose it only to have to earn it back each day? When did we transform life into a test endlessly reliant on our vital forces in order confront it?

~

And, in the end, after all these forces we attempt to seek out, draw forth, and exhaust: why bother? So as to continue and overcome life's struggles. Instead of simply confronting life's tribulations—gaze down on life from on high. Float above it all. Draw forth this vital source from out of the mud, decant it so as to grant this vitality its proper place. Its proper regimen.

~

Sirata's bounty is like a tree whose leafy branches provide shelter to those who pass by: a well quenching the thirst of a weary traveler.

SESSHIN 2007. FROM MAY 16 TO MAY 20 AT VICHY

I brought the first tome of *Sagesses Concordantes: Quatre maîtres pour notre temps*—Etty Hillesum, Vimala Thakar, Svâmi Prajnânpad, Krishnamurti along to Vichy. I've reached the chapter entitled "Looking Suffering in the Eyes." In it, these great thinkers lay bare the mechanisms of suffering and the means for remedying them. They distinguish between physical pain and suffering, the latter being nothing more than a psychic resonance of the former, produced by a spirit that refuses to accept reality. According to their collected writings, psychological suffering is the result of a denial of reality. It's a way for memory to grant a place for the continual suffering from painful events from the past. Suffering: a rumination of past suffering and the refusal to become one with reality. The past becomes delayed within the present in the form of a memory. Reading this chapter was rather instructive in helping me confront the painful but formative and edifying test of the *kiba-dachi*. Everything can provide some sort of meaning. Life has granted me the proper tools at the right moments. Somewhere Prajnanpad says: "One doesn't learn from reading books, we only learn through taking our lumps." I had just completed the luminous reading of this chapter on suffering and a couple of hours from then, after carefully anticipating it, during the special stage of martial arts training, I was going to experience it, with every square centimeter of my skin. Everything has come full circle and the training is complete.

MAY 18, 2007

This morning, the hour and a half of *kiba-dachi* went really well. The memory from last year has been erased.

~

The paths of psychological suffering are the paths of the ego.
In tossing aside the ego, one tosses out suffering.

~

Pathways: outside the struggle, far away from servitude . . .

~

Hegemonic temptation of gangrene. Taking everything, affecting everything, even the backroads. No respite.

~

Hatred is not something one eradicates from the outside but from within oneself; otherwise hate from the outside risks awakening that within.

~

These paths that I carve out are my own, even if it is not that likely I will pass back over these same grass-laden paths. Flattened from on high by my steps. These serpentine fragmented paths bear witness today that, at a certain point, I chose to seek out the fields of the countryside when winds of progress were calling me to the flourishing heart of the cityscape and that the whirlwind wanted nothing less than to sweep up everything in its path.

~

Here we set to work gaining clarity within ourselves, and subsequently a bit more clarity on the world, for we are the world.

MAY 26, 2007

Zazen is not wasting the instant.

MAY 30, 2007

Set out on a path of enlightenment. It matters little, whether it's that of Africans or the ancient Greeks, or Buddha, the Tao, Hassidism, or Christ, or Islam, or the spirits of the ancestors, through reading or writing. Each path, provided it opens onto the uninterrupted flow of life, is a path of enlightenment. Running at dusk in the direction of Saran, Montjoie, or Tête Noir: each of these is a path to enlightenment.[1]

~

Emotion is fleeting, but sentiment endures. Purified emotion becomes a sentiment. As for sensation, it does not in and of itself offer qualitative evolution. It can only allow for the possibility of a quantitative increase. Always granting more sensations. In our current age, certain organized sounds that we call music do nothing more than appeal to our sensations.

~

In spite of everything, in spite of all the spite, beneath the hail raining down in a thunderclap of denials: to believe in Humanity. Such a hope requires nothing more or less than a person worthy of this name in order to continue to believe in Humankind.

~

To traverse evil without falling for the notion that one is the incarnation of good.

~

We must be able to gain understanding even of the most abominable events, particularly those we have ourselves endured. By shedding light on a world, even a horrendous one, we can conquer it.

~

Music is one path of enlightenment.

~

"Myself alone, me and the others, the others and me, only the others. At the beginning of the path, we are swept up by it; somewhere along the way, in the middle, we carry the path itself along with us; and at the end of the path, we find ourselves lifted up." Arnaud Desjardins.

And yet, all that remains for us to traverse is the path!

~

E-motion: exiting oneself, to be driven from outside of one's center, set into movement . . .

~

Nangu: acceptance in Wolof. The opening of one's entire being to the whole. A form of rest that has a confidence in the reality manifest and that in becoming. I just read *Derniers fragments d'un longue voyage*. A magisterial work of *nangu*, of light and love.

JUNE 2, 2007

The Goal of Meditation: To rid the mind of psychic irritants such as hatred, anger, envy, pride, and jealousy. So as to allow the mind to see how reality truly is, through ripping away the veil of illusions behind which we are able to then perceive reality. So as to attain the perfection of our latent unconscious mental capacities. First and foremost: recognize one's flaws and weaknesses, and starting from there, one begins to set off on an ascending path. Purifying one's mental interior, overcoming sadness and lamentations, overcoming pain and sorrow, simply walking on a path toward peace. Once one is seated, and in remaining still, one can begin to comprehend that one's mental landscape is like the bed of a river clouded with mud; the more one learns to remain still, the more the mud slowly dissipates, and the waters slowly clear. Within a second step, one can slowly begin to remove the mud that resides at the bottom of the riverbed. Otherwise if one begins to stir and agitate the muddy depths of one interior mental river, it will inevitably cause an unwanted psychic disturbance. The body and the mind are inextricably linked, and each has an influence over the other.

Meditation is a consciousness without *ego*.

JUNE 5, 2007

On the island of Lampedusa, once winter has come and gone, fishermen snare the bodies of clandestine Africans in their nets.

~

To comprehend a truth, for the mind to truly grasp it, is one thing. To truly actualize it within one's life is entirely another.

JUNE 7, 8, 2007

I suddenly realize that the French accent *circonflexe* does not hover over the term for edge—*cime*—but gently rests, floating over the term for abyss—*abîme*.

~

Never confuse an obstacle with the insurmountable.

JUNE 9, 2007

Every act, as miniscule as it may appear, has consequences. Sometimes these consequences take time to emerge, in such a way that often we can even forget the very acts that have generated them.

JUNE 25, 2007

It has now been more than a month since I have taken up running every morning while also practicing the budo daily: the path of the Shoto. I've taken to maintaining a proper regimen: that of floating. This second *sesshin* has been a revelation. A flame has sparked within me whose presence I will want to preserve and maintain as long as possible; I feed it continuously so as to prevent the onset of entropy. It's clear that this regimen must become part of my normal routine. During this month of June, I will have worked on my *Jion*.[2] I'm slowly beginning to decipher the *Hangetsu*, a *kata* for breathing and strength whose transmission some have said was pared down and whose version we have received from Funakoshi is incomplete.

JULY 3, 2007

Occultation

For some time now, I've been looking for my copy of the Quran and I'm still not able to get my hands on it. It's hiding somewhere. For a while now, I've abandoned it for other Qurans. Is it moping somewhere?

~

I was twelve years old when I heard her voice for the first time loudly slamming against the sidewalls of my being. She wanted to free herself from the prison of her flesh.

SATURDAY, JULY 7, 2007

I set out to run around the stadium in the valley. Holding fast to the path, I wed myself to it. Such a path will turn around itself at times when it needs to. I suddenly recall the races I ran in the warmth and sand winds of Kaolack. I was thirteen years old, and I was training as a middle-distance runner with the world military champion of the 800 meters, Moussa Ndoye, who taught me to *dig down deep*. At the beginning of a race, one adopts a certain rhythm that one can maintain simply to remain at the head of the pack, Moussa explained to me. Then, I could dig deep and seek out some distance between myself and the rest of the pack, obliging the rest of them to make an even greater effort to try to catch me and reel me back in with the rest of them. Maintain one's rhythm and let the others try to catch you. When the other runners do finally ascend to your level, breathing heartily and happily, thinking that they've finally caught up with you, *dig deep* yet again, and slowly accelerate once more. Most of the time, this will discourage them from continuing since they're already running at the height of their capacities, and nine times out of ten, they will simply drop off, acquiescing to your superior ability. In Wolof, this practice is called *dogg*: to completely slice the adversary down the middle. And as I run, I still think back to my jogs on the shores of the Atlantic Ocean in Dakar, at Kaolack and Niodior. The succession of these moments compose a continuity within my psyche. The race always seems to be singular, always the same exertion of effort. Time is abolished and duration itself is established. And still today, when I run by myself, my lone adversary being nothing more than my own combat against fatigue, I still dig deep. Wednesday morning, I ran with Fahkane, my stride alongside his, and I attempted to transmit to him the knowledge of bearing witness to the effort and demands one places on oneself alone. I teach him to dig down deep, to retain a bit of his vital breath and energy for the final lap of the race.

One morning behind the administrative building of Kaolack I found myself at the starting line of a race. My mother came to cheer me on. Moussa Ndoye was there to coach me. A mixture of heat, marine air, adrenaline, and nervousness. I followed Moussa's instructions as best as I could and I won the cross-country race.

~

I love you from the bottom of my soul intoxicated by the hours still to live. I love you, calm hours of the morning, I love you, suns of stillness on the horizon.

~

Don't fall prey to illusions. Live in the instant. Be lucid and wounded.

~

Camus is a result of Nietzsche, Pascal, and Dostoevsky, of storms and bright sunlight beaming down from Tipasa, Algeria, from lightning flashes of Jean Grenier and Louis Germain.

~

To offer oneself is a natural quality of beauty.

~

Once we lived at a great crossroads, uncertain how we would earn our daily bread. This experience bestowed on us an acute awareness and sensitivity to the flux of things, pared down to the lone virtue that truly matters: the striving of survival. And yet, seeking out my daily bread was not my principal concern. Even though certain of my activities offered themselves as a way to earn money and be employed, something still resided within me that objected to merely nudging and elbowing my way through the crowds to participate in the scramble for the final breadcrumbs at feeding time. I knew that the source of life would somehow make its way to me. That the vital source would carve its path to me and that I had to remain where I was to await its arrival. This serene confidence in the generosity of life prevented me from doing everything I could, from expending all my energy to "earn a living" and assure that of my family. People thought I was irresponsible and naïve, but I merely felt I was only a dreamer among those who were even deeper in slumber. I was not ready to dig a canal to divert the river of wealth like a madman all the way to my locale. I was convinced that the ocean had already submerged the cliffs and that the waters of abundance and life would eventually find their way to my doorstep. Was it not thanks to these waters, after all, that I was alive? What then did I have to question?

～

In our discussions and within our common life, we only truly delve into a mere part of reality. For the moment, the other part of reality was too unbearable to explore. Like a half-open book, we merely content ourselves with a single page.

～

True joy does not discriminate; it does not close itself off, nor is it distributed with parsimony, nor with a precise receiver of its blessings in mind, as it's something that is not chosen; it spreads itself out, democratically, to everyone, bountiful and open; it does not withdraw into itself. In my country, a celebratory party brings everyone together, those as much known as unknown, it serves as a host for those making a brief passage through the land . . . Joy is a feeling that we don't imprison, a feeling that we don't shut away, where it would risk smothering or degenerating. The other day, the young El-ignane exclaimed to me: it's not a real party. There aren't that many people here. Joy is expansion, pain is contraction.

MONDAY, JULY 9, 2007

Not only does playing music not add to the brutality of the world, music also softens the world by way of a purified senti-ment raised to a level of incandescence.

~

An immensity of beauty surrounds us. To avoid burning our-selves, a veil, which poets sometimes pierce, separates us from such beauty.

FRIDAY, JULY 13, 2007

My Quran has reappeared. Largely based on rather miraculous circumstances. This morning I was in the middle of reading *Rumi: The Fire of Love*. A sudden desire to read verses from the Quran came over me. I then recalled that, while I no longer could find my original copy, I still had a copy of the Quran in English, with the verses written in a very tiny font making it all the more difficult to read. I immediately decided to plunge into it. Rising up from my chair, I turned, and there was the original copy of the Quran I had for so long looked for. It was on the first bookshelf of my library on the far-right wall at the entrance to my home. I must have passed by it every day with-out ever catching a glimpse of it. It must have been waiting there until I truly desired for it to finally reveal itself to me.

MONDAY, JULY 23, 2007

I note down that the words *pardon, mansuetude, clemency,* and *bounty* have all practically disappeared from spoken language. This merely means that the realities to which such words provide access have become less and less a part of our common field of experience.

SUNDAY, JULY 29, 2007

"The writer transforms a vital experience into a thing: a book. The reader takes this thing and within him it becomes life. The reader resides at another level above the writer." Jean Grosjean

WEDNESDAY, AUGUST 8, 2007

There exist melodies that feed on other melodies.

MONDAY, AUGUST 20, 2007

Always in the midst of the proper regimen: floating. This month, I've begun to decipher the Gangkaku: the crane on a rock. Wednesday morning, I return to the factory.

SATURDAY, SEPTEMBER 22, 2007

Why float? For its lightness, of course. The aerial grace of a dancer gliding through life, but above all to float like a raft helps with traversing life's myriad rivers and streams.

SUNDAY, SEPTEMBER 30, 2007

The gesture is painful and repetitive. These days in a factory are a way for me to train and practice a meditation in action. After an hour of work, I realize that my gestures become autonomized. I don't think about it any longer. The neuro-networks and connections that afford such a gesture become well-oiled. Its accomplishment no longer requires anything more than the slightest attention. And in this way, my mind and spirit are freed and suddenly become available. Often a wind blows swiftly across my mind in a somewhat obsessive way. Sometimes, it's a song that I've just heard, or it's an old wind that I've almost completely forgotten about, a tune suddenly blows forth from the depths, some old shitty song that I had heard on the radio and tried to forget and which starts pissing me off as I try to forget it again. On such occasions, I concentrate on my breath, a long and continuous exhalation and attempt to let my thoughts pass and to let go of these obsessive winds that encumber me. The challenge here is to attempt to succeed in inhabiting time in an agreeable manner in spite of the somewhat open way in which I undertake such work, even though it leads me nevertheless to desire that time pass much more quickly, and that the day's work come to an end as soon as possible. How is it possible to cultivate oneself in such a way as to become a master of one's perception of time, how can one seek to disconnect this perception from the very activity one is in the midst of performing that makes us feel a temporal passage of acceleration or slowness, its dimension of agreeability or displeasure? Several methods are at one's disposal: by elevating the rhythm of work and immersing oneself into the activity, one forgets time. In lifting one's eyes toward the hands on a clock, one is aware once again that time passes quickly. Another technique is to meditate within the activity itself, inhabit the instant independently of the effectuated gesture, and in such a manner the activity then also becomes a way of meditating. One must accept what one does. Often, what makes the passage of time miserable is some sort of refusal or rejection of what one does or a desire to live out another reality instead of fully living within one's present reality. And once again we return to the same idea of being fully attuned with what one does. Yet the most important things to first accept are the circumstances, situations, and the ineluctable and complex, yet subtle, causal chain within which our activity is situated and which leads us to the process of completing it.

～

I suddenly understood that what I should know came to me naturally. In the end, there was no need to seek out its conquest. All it took was simply to listen carefully and let it come, or rather, let it happen.

MONDAY, OCTOBER 1, 2007

To desire this as opposed to that is wanting to persist in one's being. Throughout this month of Ramadan, a time of learning and a progressive experience of effacement, of nonbeing, ending with a self-emptying, a void of self, one's true being can finally appear. Letting it flow, untangling the knots. When the ego desires one thing, one should attend to its opposite.

～

Toward what are my hastened steps moving? Where are they running? Toward nonexistence. And just as quickly, I no longer can hold on to the loop of my impatience. My steps hasten on the path. My perseverance in attending to running, right here and now, within this present existence, allows me to grant the best of myself within the exchanges I have with the glistening faces of my peers.

NOVEMBER 4 AND 5, 2007

I've been in Dakar for two days now. My parents are happy to see me, and my mother has decided to fast for three days to thank God for my safe and healthy return after all these years in exile. My brothers Sahad and Youssou are there, and I can tell they have become strong and solid, autonomous men, capable of taking care of themselves. My cousins are also at the house, Alioune Ndiaye, a young lieutenant fresh out of the National Officers School, ENOA, and Lamine Cissé, the son of Uncle Pascal, who is in his third year at the IUT in Dakar. My friend and cousin Abdou Fall is also there. My half-brothers are also present—Imam and Ahmed who are nine and seven years old, respectively. There's also Khady Diallo, my cousin, and Mami Ndiaye, a niece to my mother. Mossane went back to her mother's home. After the family reunion was over, I headed out downtown[3] with Sahad. He updated me on the political and social realities of the country. I'm taken by surprise at the acuity of his discernments. We walked from Dial-Diop to the Medina, passing Sandaga, the West Corniche, and Rue 6. I relearn how to weave through the swarm of traffic, and how to blend in with the crowds of people, inhaling some of the exhaust spewing from the cars, and rubbing up slightly against the buses. Effervescence, buzzing, density, energy, rhythm, chaos, creativity, life. I slowly rediscover the way to maneuver through all this commotion, comprising a certain flexibility, agility, and spontaneity. I rediscover sites. A handful of memories return to the surface. My eye catches a glimpse here and there of things that have been renovated by way of the perpetual flux, and others that persist in their being. I let myself be carried away a bit by the intensity and rhythm of the city. In the streets, it's the hour for the midday prayer, and a group of men assemble next to each other, kneeling on the ground, composing a community. At the end of the afternoon, I take the bus, P13 Dieuppeul, with Saliou to head over to his house at Derkhelé. We leave the quarter of Plateau. The bus passes by the Hôpital Principale, the Presidential Palace, the Place de l'Independence, l'Avenue Faidherbe, not too far from the port of Dakar, the allée du Centenaire, the Grand Mosque, and Lycée Kennedy, Colobane, HLM, Dieuppel, and finally arrive at Derkhelé. I discover the apartment that Saliou shares with his roommates and friends, and we all gather around and have a fraternal discussion. He talks to me about his life, and his projects, his current struggles. When I left he was just a budding postadolescent, and now I return to find him an adult who has fully assumed his life and attends to his conduct. In the evening, I call S. and the kids to let them know that I've arrived safe and sound and to check on them.

SUNDAY NOVEMBER 5, 6 PM

Sahad tags along with me to watch the band practice of Saliou and his group, Diaspora Groove, at Blaise Senghor. They're preparing for an important upcoming concert to be held on

November 30 at the French Cultural Center. They play beautiful music, and I can feel the profound connection between the music they play and each of the members of the group. An enthusiasm and unity of promising young talent. And yet somewhere in the back of my mind, I know that this harmony, too, will someday come to an end.

NOVEMBER 6 AND 7, 2007

I arrived at Saint-Louis around 11:30 AM. Welcomed by sand winds arising from the nearby desert, which the taxi driver taking me to Ngallèle informed me didn't truly reflect the local climate of Saint-Louis—a city of water softened by the graces of the river and surrounding sea. My uncle, Mame Cheikh Diouf, was there to welcome me and serve as my guide, helping me acclimate to the University of Gaston Berger where he teaches in the Department of Arts and Letters. He was an extraordinary help, and without him, I would have certainly had a horrible time getting settled in. I'm welcomed into his home from the very first moments. My Aunt Bintou Diop reminds me of my mother. She carries within her a great generosity and availability. She carefully watches over and attends to the minutiae that facilitate life. The administration and pedagogical team in the Economics Department provide me with a big welcome: M. Diakhaté, Mme Gueye, M. Malick Thomas . . . all of them welcome me with open arms. I'm provided an office with the assurance that the accompanying office equipment will arrive soon. My uncle insists on having an air conditioner installed. I take the shuttle between the General Secretariat's office of the UFR, the university's department of Human Resources, and the main administrative offices of the school in order to fill out all the necessary forms and begin my service at the school. It's the beginning of the year, and while some of the administration is already on site working diligently, others have yet to return. I'm told that I'll have to return tomorrow, not too early, as nobody will be there yet, but not too late, for everyone will have already left. I have yet to make the acquaintance of M. Diop, the person with whom I have to discuss my actual teaching hours. M. Lô Gueye, the director of the UFR who recruited me is not there, as he has apparently traveled to Gabon to take the CAMES examination. Soon, I will be given an apartment for my first three months here, granting me enough time to eventually find my own place somewhere in Saint-Louis. During the several days I'm attending to all the administrative details of my new job, I notice the distinct yet generous and open manner that the Senegalese people have of communicating with the other. Everyone graciously welcomes you, prays that all your affairs are carefully attended to and organized. They all try to take care of you. I quickly get the feeling that this profound attitude goes far beyond simple social pleasantries. I listen closely to the mothers walking together, *bearers of families* partaking in collective conversation. They each share their experiences without any taboos, talking through all the small things that arise. I can take a measure of the profound depths of their lived experiences. I'm struck by the sage-like benevolence and care to which their discussions lend themselves but also by the frankness and directness of their communication. Here, a cat is a cat. No need to beat around the bush. A long practice of speaking under tempered skies had accustomed me to a more self-censored form of linguistic discussion. I pay a visit to the university library. A reassuring smile creeps up the sides of my mouth in seeing that the Economics Department has all the necessary reference books on hand. I had told myself that upon settling in here I would refrain from any form of prejudice and simply observe the reality here as best as I could without coloring it. I try to apply the same exigency toward myself. This continent already gets so much bad press that often it seems even the locals end up wrongfully looking at themselves through such a deformed prism. Instead of letting myself become annoyed by certain details, I focus on all the attempts by the faculty and staff to ensure the highest quality of education for their students. Where some might see chaos, I see nothing but creativity. Next week, I have been asked to help sketch out the program requirements for both the master's program as well as the undergraduate program in economics. It feels good to actually get to participate in the creation of the foundations of the edifice. It led me smack dab into the middle of a debate about the cost of living. An increase in the price of a barrel of oil has led to an increase in the cost of other more important primary foodstuffs. The Senegalese people complain, and the first idea posited by the government to moderate inflation is to lower the salaries of the government workers. After much grumbling, the measures taken to lower government employee salaries will only concern the deputies, ministers, and the president himself. Finally, I encounter M. Diop again. He tells me I'll have to wait until the middle of November to see what courses I'll be responsible for teaching once M. Lô Gueye returns from taking the CAMES examination. Tomorrow, I head back to Dakar, where I'll make use of my time to gather up all the other required administrative materials for my employment dossier: birth certificate, a certificate verifying my morals and good standing (who's going to judge my morals and good standing?), my court records, my proof of nationality, etc. Each time a member of the faculty is Serer, my uncle is quick to let them know that I belong to the same ethnic group. And whoever it may be is always quick to ask me whether or not I speak the Serer language. When I respond by speaking in a melodious and assonant Serer, a solidarity is born that I don't want to qualify as ethnic, given the connotation of the term. Rather I would call it a connivance arising out of a natural proximity with those who partake in the same universe of reference. Kinship, *o foog olé*: a sort of primordial fraternity is realized. I feel like I'm one of their allies. But then, who would I be at war with? An electricity outage: the children continue attending to their homework by candlelight. I still have a bit of autonomy thanks to my cellphone. But I decide to stop taking notes of my impressions for the evening. It will soon be 10:00 PM, and tomorrow I have to get up at the crack of dawn.

NOVEMBER 10, 2007

I've arrived back in Dakar. Throughout the course of just one morning, I was able to obtain all the administrative documents I required thanks to the help of my father, who activated an element within his apparatus—my uncle Dethié Gueye—a Serer relative who worked at the central commissariat. The latter, who would soon be retiring, put me in contact with one of his work colleagues, who agreed to help me with whatever came up. My position within a network had begun.

Yesterday, I, Abdou Fall, Sahad, and Youssou went for a run on the East Corniche. The fermata was a night dip in the Anse cove. Four years earlier, during my previous visit, Abdou Fall, Djiby, Saliou, and I ran along this same East Corniche.

Generations renew themselves and the older ones remain. Sahad and Youssou have replaced Djiby and Saliou. They now bear the flame. In the Sarr family, all the boys carry within them this same fire and I find it reassuring. I can detect an elevated religious practice around the city, and I don't quite know what to make of it: is it a sign of social conformism, a refuge, or a luminous path? Everyone, with prayer beads in their hands, seems to be practicing the zikr, both young and old, more so the men than the women. I went to see Ablaye Cissokho at Just for U with Saliou. His album, the *griot rouge*, is of an extreme beauty. The public attending his performance, half-composed of tourists, was inattentive and very chatty and weren't at the height of the concert. Confronted with this inappropriate behavior, Ablaye Cissokho sought refuge by interacting with the other musicians. And suddenly, they immediately surrounded and supported him by performing more instrumental versions of his compositions. I understand what he's going through. When an artist offers up their heart and soul, the minimum decency that one could have is to remain attentive and listen. I had a great discussion with him after the concert. We planned another meeting soon in Saint-Louis where he also lives. In arriving back home at 2:30 in the morning, I find Sahad in the living room in the midst of practicing the zikr, prayer beads in his hands, chanting invocations.

NOVEMBER 11, 2007

This morning my mother entered my bedroom rather early and closed the window that opened onto the central courtyard of the Dial-Diop neighborhood. President Abdoulaye Wade had just paid a visit to the military headquarters of the

Senegalese army located here: all windows facing the military grounds had to be shut. For a couple of days now the military had come by and painted one of the façades of our building in the colors of the Dial-Diop neighborhood (leaving the other façades with their initial color) so the president of the République wouldn't be distracted by any vision of multicolor. All the buildings in his line of sight had to be the same color. I tried to go back to sleep after my mother's visit, but the military music blaring from the street had other ideas. These tunes, played on trumpets, where one is often left wondering if the song is really in tune, recalled the atmosphere of my childhood and adolescence spent in Senegalese military camps.

~

My mother took me to a traditional Senegalese wrestling match organized by the Serer association, Ndef Leng at the Iba Mar Diop Stadium. A total immersion into Serer culture: wrestlers competing with ardor, courage, and magnificence. Maï Ndebb, a tireless songstress of athletic chants, guides the rhythms of the wrestlers drunk off the surrounding noise that exalts their courage. Some of the wrestlers such as Papis walk slowly about as if they are in another dimension. Issa Pouye just performed a demonstration of bàkk and tuus (i song in Serer) and wants to sign up to wrestle despite being too late to do so. I can hear voices echoing from the stands proclaiming: here is a real wrestler, he's fired up and ready to rumble! Manga II, a former wrestler who has since become one of the organizers and sponsors of the wrestling association, can't resist one of the chants sung in his honor by Maï Ndebb, exalting his glory, guided by the beat of Babou Ngom's sabar drums. He stands up and graces us with a dance. Other former wrestling champions are also there. One can catch a glimpse of a firm and respectful handshake between Mor Fadam and Manga II bearing witness to their old rivalry. The soul of the Serer as well as the soul of the Senegalese amateur wrestler becomes drunk off this total immersion within the very depths of his culture. That region where the depths of his being, where his force, virility, honor, and glory awakens. Something fluid and natural serves as a bond between me and Sahal and Youssou. My long absence has meant nothing. When I left Senegal, they were two and three years old, respectively. Today, they are two big guys aged eighteen and seventeen.

THURSDAY, NOVEMBER 15, 2007

Yesterday, Abdoulaye Wade went on a vehement diatribe against the wandering merchants who anarchically set up to sell their wares on the sidewalks of the city and *who want to turn Dakar into a dump.* The city tidying campaign began at midnight. This morning, following the return of the Minister of Foreign Affairs, I walked along Place de l'Indépendence in the Dial-Diop neighborhood, walking by the avenue William Ponty and the avenue Lamine Gueye: the city was clean and there were no wandering merchants as far as the eye could see. All the gossip says that such measures won't last longer than the OCI summit that is now being organized. The *wandering merchants* in question request that some sort of space be created for them to sell their wares. They are not thieves nor are they aggressors. And they can't simply board some pirogue boats and sail off somewhere else. The merchants explain that because they are fathers of families, they must make a living somehow.

~

There is something like a social tidal wave that seeks to immerse you *illico presto* within the communal bath. And yet I resist and raise my head above the water, so as to grasp the color of the bath. I try to take advantage of this blessed time where the eye remains sharp and the gaze is still new. The old colonel has left for his final inspection at Tamba and Kolda. At the beginning of December he'll make his way to Mecca, and upon returning, he will retire after forty-four years of dear and loyal service to the Senegalese army.

FRIDAY, NOVEMBER 16, 2007

My parents are happy with my visit. And yet they don't beat around the bush. They're worried that the return of their prodigal son with a good job and a fancy diploma will only elicit jealousy and an increase of malevolent forces in the shadows. *Here, we have our own realities*, they tell me. One must carefully equip oneself. Don't do any harm to the other. Living a just life is not enough. The old colonel has prepared special purifying baths for protection against malevolent spirits that the envious can cast upon you. Since the news of my return will eventually spread, my parents try to fashion a mystical armor for me before the shadow armies arrive. They explain that I must trust in their experience. Something inside me refuses to engage in a logic of a besieged village, of fear and sentiment on the eve of battle. Is this irresponsibility on my part? A refusal to allign with a certain reality? No, quite simply I refuse to enter into a logic of defeat, fear, and tension.

SUNDAY, NOVEMBER 18, 2007

Having now been back in Senegal for more than two weeks, I find myself confronted with the country's social realities. They are complex. The country is in movement, and the Senegalese are courageous and dynamic. They believe in themselves and are resolutely turned toward the future. The *Homo senegalensis* is an interesting specimen, a mixture of Black-African culture and Muslim spirituality who nevertheless remains open to the modern world. Alongside this, they also complain about the cost of living, the poor management of the public good by the current government, which seems more concerned with its own position and internal political struggles than with the actual problems of its people. They also complain about a crisis in values (money has become the ruling value), as if the latter were not in any way their fault. The audiovisual space is endowed with several radio stations and television networks. Often, these networks and stations provide quality programming in a variety of areas and the journalists don't seem to know doublespeak. The freedom of their tone of speaking is terrifying and a measure of a healthy democratic debate, in spite of the intimidations that can be inflicted on the journalists by the regime in the country.

Yesterday, on Saturday, I went to the third edition of the Gorée Diaspora festival. Saliou and his group were scheduled to play in the village at one of the secondary venues. On the main stage, Netsayi, Afro-Soul mix, Carlou D, a new acoustic star of the country, Papa Diouf for the mbalax, Dara J, one of the best Senegalese rap groups, as well as a number of other musical acts heralding from the Antilles and the Caribbean. In parallel with the music festival, there is also a film festival showing films around exile, as well as a conference on the history of the slave trade. One can find people heralding from all over the place gathered together there on Gorée Island, people from many horizons, a lot of *toubabs*[4] and Baye Fall.[5] There is no resentment, no sense of revenge emanating from this gathering, rather the gaze is directed toward the future. An ambiance of a big village as night falls. Stars shining out over the open sea, musical vibrations, the sound of Assiko, a scintillating joy reverberating through the atmosphere. Such joy becomes mixed within me, spiced with a pang of nostalgia. I think of my ancestors that reside above and beyond these cresting waves.

TUESDAY, NOVEMBER 27, 2007

I've been back in Saint-Louis for about a week now. I'm staying in an apartment provided for teachers at the main house of the university. After several chats with the head of the Department of Economics, Monsieur Founanou, as well as with Monsieur Diaw, the lone professor with a doctorate from the UFR, and it would seem, also the scientific authority, it's decided that I will teach a course on economic development along with a course on political economy in the Masters program. I will teach a course on the recent developments of macroeconomy in the Doctoral program and a course in applied econometrics in the second semester of the Masters program. The past four days have been very intense. I had very little time to prepare the lectures for the courses in economic development and political economy, both of which I must create entirely from scratch. I finally distributed the syllabi to the students yesterday, and now I feel a great sense of relief. The message seemed to get across. The course has begun and I must tackle quite a bit of work so as to stay ahead in my preparations for teaching, so as to serenely envision the upcoming lectures. Little by little, I become acclimated, and I'm able to decipher my new environment. Upon my request, they have provided me with a somewhat more functional office. Thierno Tounkara lives across the street from me. I just met him yesterday. He is a lecturer in Paris and took a year sabbatical to come teach for free at the University of Gaston Berger. He also returned to Senegal to reenergize himself and reflect on his adventure in the West. Our journeys are similar, and the proximity of our existential experiences make it so that we understand each other before two words leave our mouths. An interesting encounter. I also met a doctoral student from the Law School who studied at the University of Orleans and who currently has an assistantship here and is continuing his dissertation in France. His name is Moustapha Aidara, a Senegalese with Mauritanian roots. The most extraordinary encounter was that I ran into a person who I was in the fifth grade with at the Collège Pie XII in Kaolack. We were friends and were both part of the English Club and the theater troupe. It had been twenty-three years since I had seen Rabi Thorpe Ndiaye. She's married and has two kids and works in Human Resources at the University. Still just as *bari affaires*.

Yesterday, I had a vision. A herd of cows passed through the campus.

THURSDAY, NOVEMBER 29, 2007

Today is a day filled with great sorrow: I received some news that really affected me. There's no way of attenuating it. The time has come to bestow on my good and joyful humor a fairly nice wallop. The lid that rattles and murmurs on the top of a pot of food where the fire burns a bit too hot. Dégonflé—a deflated ego, deflated like a veil once the wind sweeps its way through it. One must begin again and seek additional vital energy deep down within oneself, from belly to the heart, to counter the torpor seeking to install itself and take root.

After winter spring must come.[6]

FRIDAY, NOVEMBER 30

I have a meeting with Maley, the taxi driver, so he can drive me back to Dakar. Six AM in the fresh morning air at the Université Gaston Berger. The security guards debate over the progress (or lack thereof) of the Wade regime and the reasons behind its possible nonachievements. One of guards claims that the road that passes in front of the University was constructed during the time of Senghor and not Wade. Another guard doesn't agree with this assessment: "the road was constructed during the time of the colonies," he replies. A third security guard replies: "either way, it doesn't change anything. People are hungry and cannot be nourished off highways or buildings." Out on the highway, I notice that right past the Barango Auto-mechanic shop, within the shadows, one could see the swarm of talibés, for the most part barefoot, running at the side of the road like soldiers in the infantry. Where are they headed? Maley thinks they're probably heading to the Angle Tall, or to the market where the women handle and watch over all the goods. The Senegalese people are a bunch of *debaters* and *grumblers*. I have no idea who among the French or Senegalese bestowed such a noble demeanor onto their

Senegalese compatriots. In the *seven seats* that are all heading to Dakar, everyone defends their interests, their comfort, and firmly negotiates the additional costs for transporting their luggage. The *elegant woman* seated behind me refuses to let anyone place a sack of dried fish beside her. The strong odors emanating from it risk coalescing with her fine attire *that she already spent a long time perfuming.* Society constantly self-normalizes and self-educates. We debate everything. We talk about the latest changes made by Wade, about the guerilla warfare of the tidying campaign waged on the *wandering merchants in the city* who pushed back the decision made by the government . . . etc. In each situation, each individual formulates his or her own point of view and proposes a solution that they believe is best adapted to the situation at hand. The tone is often resolute and authoritative, but the ambiance remains respectful—like good little children. The Senegalese comprise a society of individuals. The initial illuminations bask in the sky above, and the blueish-orange hues are reflected in the waters of the river below. The Sahel is there, dry and majestic. Several trees are spread out in the middle of the grassland already sporting their pale ochre coats.

FRIDAY, DECEMBER 7, 2007

My father must depart for Mecca tonight at ten. At the last minute his departure is pushed up to 1:00 PM. So I find myself on the road from Saint-Louis to Dakar at 2:35 AM. Maley, the taxi driver, picks me up and we set off. I carefully explain to him that if we want to continue our collaboration that he must be punctual. Yesterday, we had agreed that he'd pick me up in front of UGB at 2:00 AM sharp. I ask him to give me an idea of how much the trip will cost. He refuses to offer any suggestion of a price. He tells me that it's up to me to decide. The main thing being that we *nu jàppante*—literally that we hold strong, that we solidify a lasting relationship together. I reply that he still has to give me an idea of how much it will cost, that I don't have any idea how much the gas will cost to get to Dakar from Saint-Louis. He provides me the information but leaves me alone with my casuistry. The Senegalese society is hierarchical—it's within its very psychological structure. One thing is clear: we don't recount the fable of equality. Perhaps we should seek to actively sow the dream of equality with regard to rights. Everyone consents to their place and fully occupies it. In this light, semiotics is important. Every individual emits signs indicating their rank, social position, birth, filiations. Doors open or close depending on *who you are.* When one has chosen simplicity as an existential attitude, one feels a certain annoyance upon being conferred a certain status and all the attributes that go along with it. When one interacts with you by way of deference and sometimes even with a certain obsequiousness. Conversely, as soon as you object to occupying the place that has been attributed to you within the hierarchy, it is interpreted as an authorization made to familiarity and the triviality of relations. As such, within this structure of the *dominant/dominated* we end up accepting to be the *dominant* while still attempting to avoid it, whether or not it's our conscious that dictates (suggests) such a choice to us, the arrogance and contempt that inevitably lingers around the folds of our lips and watches over the style of our pouts.

On the road to Dakar, I listen to *Soutouro* by Ablaye Cissoko, *Seey* by Niominka-bi, *Stepping out* by Steel pulse, *Epitaphe en Fa* by Andère, and *Avec le temps* by Leo Ferré.

I arrived in Dakar at 6:30 AM. At the house, I find my aunts, Mariama Sarr—my father's older sister—and Maama Ndoye. Here, the greetings are an ethos (an ethics). They bid me welcome and proffer some beautiful words, and inquire into my health and that of my family and neighbors in far-off Saint-Louis, and of the others I've seen. They express good intentions toward their child and the human being that I am. They formulate wishes for peace, prosperity, and longevity. Within such a speech act, the information provided matters less than the cathartic virtue of the Word that does both the liver and the body good.

SATURDAY, DECEMBER 15, 2007

Finally. Huge drops of sweat no longer pour from me every time I take a couple of steps. My metabolism has finally re-adapted to the Sahelian climate. My way of using language and my outer shell as well, I surprise myself about how stubborn I can be regarding the typical negotiations with taxi drivers and others vendors in the purchase of goods. It's strange; old reflexes return as if awaking from a long sleep. Like an old rucksack we had forgotten how to use, and for which time had softened its straps, widened its pockets, and tanned and hardened its burlap.

Love is a wound. Its taste derived from the sweet-sour juices of the *maad*. The weda fruit from the Casamance, brimming with a reddish-brown sugar. It is a possible never fully realized. A mourning from the very day of its birth.

The deafening echo of this cavern condemned *ad vitam aeternam* to remain a vast abyss.

WEDNESDAY, DECEMBER 19, 2007

Life is going on. Rivers to cross, challenges, joy, pain
But
Peace is coming, slowly but deeply.[7]

THURSDAY, DECEMBER 20, 2007

I look out at the world from here. This new perspective fundamentally changes things. From now on, I will only perceive the world through my eyes alone, and behind my eyes, from those of my ancestors.

THURSDAY, DECEMBER 27, 2007

I've been back in Orleans for a week. I've come to pay a visit to my family. The children weren't aware that I was coming. I could almost measure the sudden radiant joy that was unleashed by my unexpected arrival. I come bearing packages of energy that I hoped would be capable of reinvigorating the family tiding them over and keeping them steady until the summer. Here, it's winter. It's cold, but above all, the vibrations in the air are of a poor quality. The hearts are emitting a very low frequency. A community is crumbling, a generalized desolate feeling of panic. My brother, O Youngatt, the one who keeps company, deserves his name. He carefully looked after my tiny family. This community needs more bearers of good tidings. People who assume the difficult and thankless task of *religare* when egos and cowardice dis-unify and cut the ties that had been patiently and carefully woven. I'm still saddened to see how quickly such a gangrene can render rotten everything in its path.

This morning, before heading out for a run, Ali Dioune, the *witness*, stopped by to see me. In spite of the joy of our encounter, I can sense his disappointment in not having succeeded in getting me to join his cause. He must think that he didn't have enough time at his disposal to complete his mission. Ali, the tenacious one, doesn't give up. He suggests I install Skype on my computer at Saint-Louis so we can continue our *discussion*.

I run around the stadium in the valley. My strides regain the fresh pink track where I had been able to exhaust my fatigue these past several years. In the fog of winter, the path under my feet is clear and relaxed. Even the column of bushes on the edge of the track has been manicured. Under the trail created by my strides another long path appears where I can make out vast prairies and crevices. Knowing which way one is going radically changes the tempo and rhythm of things. I slowly and profoundly effectuate gestures of the budo. My steps are no longer in a hurry. Resolutely, from now on, they merely fall into place.

JANUARY 24, 2008

Sometimes, social life here takes on the image of the roads: full of potholes one must avoid.

But there are moments when everything aligns itself. And a sudden peace arises. From the tips of one's toes, it penetrates the very foundations of one's being. In such moments, a feeling of gratitude emerges: gratitude for existence, the heavens, for the universe, the orishas, for God.

MARCH 23, 24, 25, 2008

Elevating one's heart rate, holding fast to the street, to the paths, to the concrete: to run through a city. I love this way of discovering cities. Discovering the streets, the buildings, the dead-end streets, the flourishing patios: making use of one's arms and legs throughout the vastness of open space.

Here, everything is clean and smooth, even the revolt is reserved for special areas with well-designed posters. It is not overflowing. The posters give off an allure of advertisements for laundry detergent. On a background blue as the ocean: "OMC stop the subventions for fishing." It is this somber characteristic that gives life and movement to a painting that is all too neat and tidy.

A DAY OF ALLOTTED TIME

Springtime has arrived. Naïssan is here. Primrose and Daffodils . . .

My Helvetia, with her heart of a Nubian princess, her body with an aurora of the Nile: twenty thousand cantons traversed in pilgrimage by my burning heart. A pilgrimage to the Mecca of Love. Medina is beautiful, but one must still follow the return path. The path which flows back to the source. To the source of everything. To the source of Love.

The soul retains an indelible impression from its passage to paradise. The depths of one's gaze are forever affected by it. Touched by a halo of light, which from then on refracts the shadows of the world.

Climbing up Mont Salève. Snow is falling in silence. Peace. Nothing but peace. Peace, peace.

ONE DAY, A MAN FROM
THE ISLAND OF NIODIOR
TOLD ME SO!

Whoever listens learns
Thus is known what you didn't know.
So you make another knowledge from what you already knew.
As for what you thought you knew, you have finally journeyed
    out of a long night.

OF TRUTH

Know truth, but only utter it at a time when it is useful.
For always speaking little truths prevents the great ones from
    living.

~

There are ways of demonstrating that we know we are right
    that make us lose such benefits.

~

To grasp the truth of the instant.
To grasp the truth in movement.

~

Your inner truths: assume them, live them, silence them.

HUMANS . . .

Do you see them precipitating toward the gates of the new
temples, exchanging gold for chimeras?

~

Supposedly living for the sublime, dogs that tear each other
apart.

~

They exhibit the weight of the burdens they bear. Do they
take them to be crowns?

~

Their age bears wrinkles and white hair, sometimes
bitterness and regrets. Age doesn't necessarily rhyme
with Sage.

~

The human. Not all paths lead there.

CURIOUS AGE . . .

It's a curious age ours, where freedom is to be a slave to one's
    instincts and desires. Where pleasure is a tyrant that
    softens and oppresses!

~

It's a curious age, where tolerating the other is to not
    recognize them.

~

Curious age, where intelligence is knowing how to be on the
    good side,
Where impudence is daring to let one's soul cry out,
Where kindness is a profitable business.

~

Curious age, where the players who refuse to cheat are
    excluded from the game.

~

During the era of the advertising firm, poets rent out their
    rhymes to Mir and Atlantis as they dock alongside each
    other.

~

It would seem that the great work of man has been achieved.
    Humankind attained its apex with the cloning of Dolly.

~

And yet, the troubadours of yesteryear will finally rediscover the ephemeral life, here, as the greatest of human works yet still futile, when it no longer remains the great task at hand.

OF VIRTUE

The first man who entered into *hell* was a being conscious of
his virtue and drunk on his piety.

~

The first man who entered into *paradise* was a being who
refused to go there alone.

~

Constraint alone does not wring vice from one's soul. At
best, it merely adds another layer: cowardice.

~

They desire the Absolute. Immaculate, I must avoid the dirt.

~

A Virtue only exists by its very lack of self-awareness.

OF TEMPTATION

Yesterday, temptation took the face of someone who was
  forbidden.
You can look, but you cannot touch.
You cannot even look, lower your gaze!
You can smell but you cannot taste!
Must I also pinch my nose closed?

~

I partook of the forbidden fruit; they claim I have sinned!
Strange, I feel no sense of remorse.
How can I therefore repent?

OF PATIENCE

It slowly draws forth the fragile blade from out of the
    narrow sheath.
It is the clear water that breaks against the rocks in the
    early morning hour.

A gentleness that revives a smile on the face of an ogre, a
    spark flowing
From one twig to another twig until it has become an ardent
    yet fiery furnace.

It is the stone transformed into an impregnable tower.
The dream that leads to the end of the trail on the paths
    of *Miramas.*

The impatient one, who at midnight sets out to find the sun
    in the Southern Hemisphere, will see nothing of the sun
    of patience that rises and illuminates one's very soul.

From night, he will embark toward night.
Throne of courage,
    nothing resists such sweet corrosion.
Run back toward patience,
    since patience is the very force of the gods!

FATE

You cultivate this field of preestablished limits.
The harvest of two seasons offers you providence after
    dearth.

Fruit of your faith, of your passion, your labor,
fate is the shadow of your will.
May the sun radiate upon it at the highest of Zeniths and
    lowest of celestial Nadirs.
May it only be smaller or greater.

If the movement of the sun does not depend on your will,
It is still a result of your good will
    That these rays of light encounter their shadow
At the hour when the sun burns its brightest.

YOU

Your virtue, is it such a heavy weight to bear that you make
me support it like this?

～

Your pride, a flame that you spark yet do not know how to
put out.

～

Your satiety, my hunger.

～

Stop, sleep, awaken: speak with other words and you will see
with other eyes.

～

Aspire for something better. Live your destiny.

～

Uncompromising with oneself and tolerant toward the other:
not the other way around.

～

When was it that you decided to put on your mask and await
death?

～

Escape from your claustration and dare to live.

OF ART

Horrible my suffering would be if it plucked away my senses
for contemplation.

~

Life is worth living, this twilight falling onto the valleys of
the Arcies, Ewi, distilling her melodies, as Ewi from
yesteryear.

~

When I hear people say: "I would like to make a living from
my art," I reply: "I can do nothing but live with my art. It
is a necessity that lives, inhabits, and grows at the core of
my solitude."

~

Art is a passage from a state of nonmanifestation to a state of
manifestation.

~

Artists don't justify themselves. The artist alters the degree
of the existent. Henceforth: the world must include it.

~

Time: an eternity rendered invisible.

~

Ruby red, wild fruit, vase of promises, suave barbaric
enclosures.
Fire. Life.

~

Poetry has a price (that one must pay). Solitude, falling
to one's knees, accepted suffering and all of it firmly
endured.

~

To monetize beauty, what a loss!

BETRAYAL

It will catch up with you at the surest of moments.

~

A man of honor betrayed me.
Strange that he didn't perform hari-kiri upon himself.

~

Raise yourself up and have contempt for their betrayal. At
the next chance of a kiss grant yourself the confidence to
grant your heart to whomever speaks to it!

OF JUSTICE

With one single cry of freedom, the wall of oppression
   begins to crack.

~

We are guilty of dependency.

~

I partitioned out my treasure into four pieces, offering
   two portions to the peasant and two to the lord. I was
   equitable and the share was just.

COVETING

I covet no other empire than myself.

THE PATH

The masters of chatter harangue the crowd and show the way.
Alone on the path of your profound conviction, you journey.

～

You will not find it among any parchment.
It will reveal itself to you, if you know how to uplift the
    various pieces that compose your soul.

～

Your way is a path that was never borrowed, a tall grass that
    awaits your steps to flatten it down.

VICTORY

Any victory is only ever a victory over oneself.

~

To vanquish is also to vanquish the bitterness and dejection
of defeat.

~

To vanquish is also triumph over triumph.

~

Evil's victory is to have persuaded us that the good has
become impossible.

LOYALTY (FIDELITY)

It rarely resides where one thinks.
It is neither a prairie where everyone crowds nor a debt owed
to the multitude.
It is a backroad, lesser traveled that finds its morning hour
within the freshness of one's own gaze.
Every loyalty is first a loyalty to oneself.
Never be loyal to the other but remain loyal to your own
inner truths.
Such truths are the daughters of time, that dance and change
according to the seasons.
May fidelity be your companion, even if for her, you must be
unfaithful to the world.
Do not fear transgression since transgression is often to see
beyond the edge of the forest.
It's often in this manner that one can find one's way back
onto the path of authenticity.

SELF

If my peace is here, my path is here.

~

Here, now, profoundly, intensely, definitively.

~

Dare great heights. Endure great heights.

~

Dare to attain self-accomplishment.

~

I made my way down into the arena. It was perhaps better to remain in the stands, so I return to my seat.

~

To be born, to strip oneself bare, and become reborn. To be.

~

There is no worse solitude than not being able to share one's pains, save for not being able to share one's joys. This torrent of happiness that we are obliged to retain within us then becomes oppressive, stifling.

~

Do we herald from where we are born? From where we die? From the interstices?

~

The various states of the soul fluctuate and change. Wait.

~

The essential is inalienable.

~

If I must love you, then let me love you freely. Otherwise, you
are a Tyrant. And I can't love a Tyrant.

~

I am unable to enter into the house of prayer with reverence,
fervor, and humility. I will remain at the door.

~

You told me, he told me, they told me: I listen to the
fathomless oceanic depths of my soul.

~

Kill the weak part of generosity.

~

The Word was bestowed upon me as both grace and burden.
I was refused speech. Abrupt language and a narrow
throat. Of Demosthenes, I have dreamt, my will has
liberated it, my chant has rendered this word sublime.

~

To attain that which is permanent.
Since nothing is permanent and collapses into movement.

~

In the depths of night, we are all blind.

～

Cities where I cannot peacefully stroll along the sidewalks. Bulldogs and German Shepherds pull me away from my sweet slumber.

～

Friendship saves fixed ideas. The love one draws from attraction to gravities.

～

There is no barbarism that isn't weighed down by civilization.

～

Neither resentment, nor guilt: to continue one's oeuvre with exigency, perseverance, and calm.

～

As one climbs, one can be nothing more than a ladder.

～

Every patricide is a tyrannicide.

～

During periods of calm, it is wise to gather together the provisions of one's energy. Life will certainly offer up some asperities.

～

To travel along on a razor's edge, resolutely, in balance. The capacity of one's load is maximal. One additional gram of weight and one falls into the abyss. During such a moment, it's best to not carry the other on one's back.

~

When a room has light shone upon it, its dust also becomes visible.

~

The freedom of a lighthouse is for its light to burn out.

UNINTERRUPTED

DEVELOPMENTS . . .

A leaf swirls about dancing in the wind and falls to the ground. Life is this time between such a caesura and an inevitable collapse onto the wet ground of plowable earth. A knight from the Middle Ages who does not understand that one makes so much hay because a man simply wants the hand of a woman. A gentleman clad in iron clothes will run like eight horses and with the capacity of traversing three hundred kilometers in 3 hours and 15 minutes, his foot pressed hard against the ground. A being who feels the essential and fragile vibration of his life: organic, sensitive, biological, social, cosmic.

A being writes and bears witness to his life experience, the outcome of his solitude, the latter being something that can be transformed into a life for the one who can incorporate it; enduring himself thusly, reinforcing himself, and in this way proceeding from everything, recognizing his mortality, confronting the mystery and the unknown that lies in front of him.

A man retaining a foreknowledge of his life. Aspiring to slow down thanks to a wound bestowed upon him by lucidity. A man at the crossroads of all paths, a man out of synch, a man *out of joint.*

The winds batter me. The rains serve to bathe me for days on end. Driver ants pace up and down the cracks in my bark through the grooved paths they cut out. Magpies make nests on my arms. Sometimes the back of a passerby, an axe blade, the fresh desire of lovebirds, immobility is my station. I cannot save myself from danger, my survival depends exclusively on the well-meaning care of my brothers from the kingdom of the living. Death has its sights set on me from all sides. From the air above, it takes the name of lightening. From the ground, it comes in the form of the butcher's axeblade or a sawblade or a chainsaw. The station I have acquired within this life is that of acceptance.

I have suddenly become weary. I shall rest until tomorrow.

~

At dawn, a shallow breeze gently disrupts the conformity of my leaves upon which I write. The depths of the earth rise up within the sap that nourishes me. From my arms the magpies take flight toward their azure pastures. The driver ants still crawl along my trunk, their heads bent down toward the ground.

The virtue of wisdom, whether carried by the saint or the madman, the writer or the artist, is to help one to live in the *hic et nunc*. The rest . . . blah, blah, blah, . . . blah!

To sit beauty down on its knees, like an errant friend, to find it bitter and insult it. A profound peace is a much more preferrable ruler than the servitude imposed by beauty. Is it of this world? Yes, reply the enlightened ones: the four noble truths, increase the path eightfold, the three refuges . . . to sum it up: a quest and retrieval. Hum! All this is very fine and well, but what is in store for the dilletantes? A sudden opening onto everything . . .

The pupils follow the traced words that crash into each other at the end of the line. Signs that make sense within an ever-growing consciousness, breasts that toss about with the warm blood of a life.

Grant me peace, it matters little when it arrives, *na jaar fimu war a jaar*, for lives and lives, may they culminate in an extinction of craving and in a nonreturn: *parinirvana*.

For a long time, I have preferred happiness to wisdom; to renounce happiness seems to me nevertheless an even greater wisdom, but alas I continue to prefer happiness to wisdom. To renounce happiness still seems to me to be an even greater wisdom. All it takes is a step. To the side. The sky above is there to bear witness to a luminescent solitude.

The Tavern has closed its doors. Amina has left for Morocco, I don't know what's happened with Souad. As for Kiné, she has returned to Dakar. This long, looming corridor opening onto a courtyard beneath an open sky where we drink tea with Moro, Silla, and Doudou has placed the key under the doormat. The concerts of Maama Sadio in an indescribable ambiance, the unique and imperial sound of Ngam's guitar. The subtle beats of Tapha, the drummer. Bécaye's groove—the bassist with trapezoidal glasses. The wandering sleepwalkers Maurice Ndiaye and Mbaye Sarr, the former military officer, still *ethylized* but still extra-lucid; perhaps they have attained the state of superconscious sought after by Sri Aurobindo. Mbaye Sarr, a monumental intelligence confined and reduced to an educational institution. The confluences are there only for a very short time. A site closes. And all the rivers begin to take back up their currents. Souls disperse and begin to seek out new sites to cling to, new spaces of coalescence.

~

She gazes out at love from afar. She consents to it moreso by apprenticeship to an incontestable given rather than by passion. She tries her hand at it as one participates without much conviction in one of the myriad games of the city; and one day, in confronting such a game, she seeks to pay tribute to it, to learn all its tricks, mimics, secrets, and abysses . . .

~

When adults refuse to grow up and endlessly go looking for another father, they create a God the father with all the attributes of a patriarchal tribal chief.

~

Three-fourths of the phone calls I receive are in no way curious as to what I'm up to, as to how I'm really doing, nothing at all to do with a simple question of care and concern for the other. A myriad of solicitations, requests, expectations, sometimes even recriminations . . . Sometimes, I tell myself that if I isolated myself from the hordes I'd feel better, that I'd recharge myself and overflow with an abundance of energy. As time goes by, commerce has become all the more utilitarian, a practice greatly lacking *convivio*, and this seems to be all the more the case once this newfangled electronic bracelet that is the cellphone has entered into our everyday lives.

Where is the love to be found instead of concrete jungle?[1]

~

To write in silence, with an assonant language that the book renders deaf. Silence is not the total absence of sound but the presence of sounds that are not so chatty.

~

I'm in a place that could be said to resemble paradise as described in the Quran: filled with gardens and rivers flowing down below . . . *khali-dina fiha*. I'm reading *Une saison en enfer.*

All that is missing are the seductive houris with seashells in their eyes. "As long as I can recall, my life has been a banquet where all hearts open themselves up wide, and from which all wine flowed. One evening, seated on the knees of Beauty—and which I found fairly bitter—and I insulted her." On this morning in the paradise of Djilor, where the manatees come to drink from the spring of Simal, I write to a friend the following lines:

My dear friend,

I'm writing you this letter on the banks of one of the tributaries of the Saloum river. I arrived here yesterday evening around 7pm. I stopped for the evening at a friend's house, Anne Catherine Senghor, who takes care of a literary and eco-lodging site called "La source aux lamantins." Today, I continue on my way to Niodior. It's a magnificent place. From time to time, the sun pierces through the mangrove and the tree canopy and I'm forced to squint. All the noise of nature is present, in all its phenomenological splendor. Nothing but pure sound, stripped bare of signifying intent. I begin to think that such a simple relation with our environment has become a luxury. I feel that you will not easily abdicate and that, as Nietzsche states, you will not be satisfied by an answer that is "great like a smack in the face." Moreover, that's not even the goal, to make you abdicate anything whatsoever. I love your exigency in all things. Remaining a disciple of your own comprehension of things appears like a just path. It's merely a question of indicating (sharing) the paths that others have taken in order, at the end of these paths, to find some kind of peace. Perhaps these paths will satisfy you? Perhaps you need to trample down and flatten out the tall grass of your own path. Camus says in Noces that

it's a question of undertaking the geography of a certain des-
ert. And this singular desert is only sensible for those who can
reside there without deceiving their thirst, and this is only due
to the fact that they populate the waters with happiness. Yes, I
can feel the effects of a positive karma. :-)

See you soon.

~

Bobin, Dany, Bachir, Rodney, Boris . . .[2] whomever it may be, the person I'm currently reading always occupies my thoughts. For the hospitality to be complete, I must let them depart, head off on their way, get their affairs in order and regain their time; all that will remain from their time spent with me is one last flower from a final bouquet. The flower I will gather from him will contain the concentrate of the best sap that he will have transmitted to me.

~

Here, high above the rooftop, so as to balance the overflowing vitality of the flock of children of the Boussoura by way of a fruitful silence, I need a room where the air, light, and sounds of pure nature can enter freely. A large wooden worktable from the country. A bed for taking naps and for love. A dry rug and a zafu, some incense, a bowl and a kesa. The company of several good philosophers, a mystic and a poet, a novelist, *my favorite things, sira, soutouro, nateikha* . . .

~

Since daybreak, they have been chatting: calmly and gently. It has been three months since they've found themselves in the midst of a peaceful morning, on this island that watched over their birth more than fifty years ago, now. At their age, at this moment in their life, reunions are had in order to converse peacefully. Thus pleasure makes itself available.

~

This morning, I decided to reopen an entryway into the most profound interiors of my life, and as a consequence, perhaps, I also shut the door on other promising paths. In spite of my reticence, I've decided to have one more go at a positive rearticulation for a passion that had somehow lost its steam. A vital breath that had suddenly vanished and changed locations; perhaps that's where it will reside from now on, as refreshing as ever. Preeminence of the known over radical novelty? I hesitate still. I've stored this message that conceals such a return within my skull, and in so doing, in delaying its departure, it leaves me with these moments replete with possibilities before the plunge. I don't know what the consequences will be of actions that I'm prepared to take in the coming weeks. I weigh how much the choices we make always have a portion of their composition that resides in the shadows.

~

There is a story about the lands held by the family of Mbine Samba. The grandparents and the great uncles helped themselves to them without thinking one minute about us, all of us others who lived away from the countryside in the city. Upon such occasions, those who are absent are always wrong. They cultivated gardens close to A PECC and then made use of the remaining land for their crops. They simply decided that, of the remaining portions of the land, no gardens would be granted to anyone else. My father requested that we be re-turned our rights, those of us who can't cultivate any gardens, we will be doomed. My father said: either they let us partake of the fruits of their gardens or grant back to us a portion of them. When it's a story about land, men always rise to their feet. My Uncle Birama Koûria, my father, and I went to the piece of land where my father had already sketched out the portion he would take back. I walked between them, standing a head-length taller, and they stood taller still in their convic-tions to not let things be. As we arrived at the site, between the baobabs, the "neews" and the land of those from Damaal, my father defiantly blurted out: "I'm going to take a big piece of land." There was an easement right in the middle of the land that, at a glance, appeared to be at least 150 steps long. Later that week, cement posts—demarcating the boundaries of the space all the more—would be installed. For the moment, one could still easily remove the wooden stakes demarcating the partitioning.

Making our way back out of the area, we passed by the littoral in front of the baobab inhabited by the genie/spirit o ngonoli. This entity liked for men to walk by on a Friday afternoon. He liked to tempt each of them by way of their most secret desires. To one of them he mirrored the image of prayer mats; to another he displayed images of clothes. My father and uncle recalled larger-than-life stories about that tree. Those who cut wood from it and carried it back home saw their houses immediately burn down. Sometimes, the spirit would leave folded money on the ground near the tree, and those walking by would avoid touching it. An American in the Peace Corps, who took the name of Idy Ndong and who had disobeyed some of the rules, lost his mind and was sent back home. The spirit *o ngonoli* even got his claws into the old Saliou. One day my grandfather was tending his field and accidentally set fire to part of it. He fell gravely ill. While we all set about to tend to him and heal him, every evening *o ngonoli* would come to Bousoura, sit on stool next to the bed of Maama Ami, who took care of the old Saliou, and told her: *Bo neen rek* (will things remain as such?) Which meant: did I really lose part of my sanctuary? Will I not be compensated? A myriad of millet cakes and libations, victuals of all sorts were granted as an offering in order that the spirit might forgive the offense made to him. Soon after, Maama Saliou got better and recovered.

Niodior has changed, both my uncle and my father tell me. The folks who live here have chased the spirits of place into the forest little by little. For a long time, they lived alongside each other—respecting each other's territory. But progressively, the townspeople conquered the spaces of the spirits.

~

Words or sayings that have lost their fruitfulness. Rehashed, and endlessly recounted, chanted for centuries, years, months, days, and hours via all sorts of media, several times a day, as if they had to constantly reassure themselves of their existence. A form of speech that the majority of those who hear it believes serves to scare them into preserving a faithfulness to a past covered over by the ashes of time. That they must deny time, radical novelty, the novel flow of the arriving days. Words that claim to have "said it all" about everything that has been said. A type of speech that arrests the creative function of language: to name what is, and what is forever emerging, what doesn't cease being born. A series of words that has no other intention than recitation: a repetition that, after a certain time, exhausts its virtues. A form of speech that becomes rotten as soon as it no longer claims to echo the very intimate and profound heart of man. We say that speech or words fall to the earth from the heavens, and through their acceptance without any reservations, they force the spirit to bow by way of their precedence.

A series of words or phrases heralding from some ancient wisdom lacks a wisdom of the present.

~

Hawlaane Noor Frances Sarr-Robbins is a name that could have come right out of the pages of a novel by Toni Morrison: a saga about a Black family from the nineteenth century, an owner of a *hacienda* in Latin America. But it's merely the name of one of my nieces. Her father is a Black American who found himself an African tree worth his liking, my younger sister. Hawlaane is therefore an African American in the most replete sense of the term. Already at the age of seven she possesses the practical sense of Americans. She optimizes all her actions. Her mother plans on sending her back to Senegal as soon as possible, so Hawlaane can continue with her development of roots. Several weeks in the summer spent here in Senegal between the village and the city, reintegrating her into a new fabric of sensations, significations, and sounds and images stored away in the back of her mind that we hope one day will reemerge with a splendor and that will help to shape the creole hybridity of her life's path.

IMPRESSIONS FROM THE FASO,[3]
SEPTEMBER 11, 2011

Bobo Dioulasso. The Red Earth of the Faso.

A great bustling swarm of thousands of souls riding on scooters, disciplined men and women riding within a movement of traffic that is not that tumultuous. They all share in the same gesture: here, or in Dakar, or New York City, one catches a glimpse of someone constantly pulling up their low-cut jeans, sitting at the waist yet somehow still remaining tight . . . but which endlessly fall down—sometimes leading one to catch a suggestive glimpse of the man or woman's underwear beneath. This fashion trend has become a mania of the erotic gesture: a truly global trend. And yet, what is more elegant, more noble, more mysterious than wearing an African *pagne*, the delicate wrap dress? The girls from the south—from Abidjan, Niamey, Bobo, and Dakar—besides attending to this gesture, also murmur the same sweet words from corny B-series television shows imported by satellite from the West, dreaming of the same amorous plots as those found in Brazilian or Indian soap operas. Everywhere: the same uniformization of the expressions and examples of the taste of the other. The same impoverishment of signs of the body and soul. Perhaps they even partake in the same simulated expressions for ecstasy; onomatopoeia gleaned from films shown late at night and forbidden to those under sixteen years of age. At the heart of this culture impoverished by an unbridled mimicry, knocking at the doors of the most intimate part of self, the girls from our countries no longer even know how to express themselves and their voluptuousness in their own native tongues.

A university campus sits several kilometers outside of the city, on the edge of a green space, created to stave off the desertification of the Sahel and rejuvenate the landscape. It's the site of an inter-university doctoral program bringing together all the top students who stayed on the continent heralding from eighteen different countries. The participating professors listed also herald from all over the continent to tend to these promising young minds in order to plant new seeds into the earth for a new day of hope to arrive. The message must be crystal clear: there is no time to waste. Such is the educational mission statement.

L'hotel Auberge, where we are staying, is a remnant of past glory. Walls with paint flaking off, a building of resistance, filled with old rotary phones one might find in a painting by Andy Warhol. And yet, one morning, in returning to the main floor, a light shone down onto an ochre stone with such an old-fashioned gleam that its instance touches you. Such a discreet glimpse of beauty doesn't yield itself so quickly. Once the lively incandescence of the illumination of the minds who partake in and animate it are added together, the windows of their consciousness open up on it in a sudden comprehension: the abnegation of a functionary, the kindness of a receptionist gather together all the requisite ingredients for a joy that gently climbs up the staircase of one's being.

A sudden downpour instantly transforms the streets into a torrent of red tears. For a moment, life becomes a painting. A life-size watercolor. The streets bleed red at the feet of green-hued trees beaten down by the monsoons of September. Impressions from an austere and honest Faso that begins to bloom and silently grow.

TRANSLATOR'S NOTES

African Meditations

1. *Mi hé réta* refers to the Serer language for "I'm leaving."
2. The author is referencing Francis Cabrel's song "Comme eux." The lyrics referenced in French are: "Rien que de la lisse surface / Que du collant double face / Ho, fasse le ciel qu'on soit comme eux."
3. "Avec le temps, avec le temps va, tout s'en va, on oublie le visage et l'on oublie la voix, le cœur quand ça bat plus c'est pas la peine d'aller chercher plus loin, faut laisser faire et c'est très bien . . ."

Journal of My Hastened Steps

1. The author is referring to his running route through various neighborhoods in and around Orléans, France.
2. Jion is a reference to an entire series of martial arts *kata* practiced in Shotokan style of karate.
3. English in the original.
4. *Toubab* is a common West African term for Westerners or people of European decent.
5. The Baye Fall are a prominent religious sect in Senegal.
6. English in the original.
7. English in the original.

Uninterrupted Developments . . .

1. English in the original.
2. The author is referring to the writers Christian Bobin, Dany Laferrière, Souleymane Bachir Diagne, Rodney St. Eloi, and Boris Boubacar Diop.
3. Burkina Faso.

A UNIVOCAL BOOK

DREW S. BURK, CONSULTING EDITOR

Univocal Publishing was founded by Jason Wagner and Drew S. Burk as an independent publishing house specializing in artisanal editions and translations of texts spanning the areas of cultural theory, media archeology, continental philosophy, aesthetics, anthropology, and more. In May 2017, Univocal ceased operations as an independent publishing house and became a series with its publishing partner, the University of Minnesota Press.

Univocal authors include:

Miguel Abensour
Judith Balso
Jean Baudrillard
Philippe Beck
Simon Critchley
Fernand Deligny
Jacques Derrida
Vinciane Despret
Georges Didi-Huberman
Jean Epstein
Vilém Flusser
Barbara Glowczewski
Évelyne Grossman
Félix Guattari
Olivier Haralambon
David Lapoujade
François Laruelle
David Link
Sylvère Lotringer

Jean Malaurie
Michael Marder
Serge Margel
Quentin Meillassoux
Friedrich Nietzsche
Peter Pál Pelbart
Jacques Rancière
Lionel Ruffel
Felwine Sarr
Michel Serres
Gilbert Simondon
Étienne Souriau
Isabelle Stengers
Sylvain Tesson
Eugene Thacker
Antoine Volodine
Elisabeth von Samsonow
Siegfried Zielinski

Felwine Sarr is an economist, novelist, and philosopher. He holds the Anne-Marie Bryan Chair in the Department of French and Francophone Studies at Duke University and was named by *Time* magazine among the world's one hundred most influential people in 2021. His works include *Afrotopia*, *Dahij*, and, most recently, the groundbreaking report *The Restitution of African Cultural Heritage: Toward a New Relational Ethics*, cowritten with Benedicte Savoy.

Drew S. Burk has translated more than a dozen works of continental philosophy and theory from French, including *Afrotopia* by Felwine Sarr and *The Unconstructable Earth: An Ecology of Separation* by Frédéric Neyrat, which won the 2019 French Voices Award First Prize for translation. He is the editor of the Univocal series with the University of Minnesota Press.

Souleymane Bachir Diagne is professor of philosophy and Francophone studies at Columbia University. He is author of numerous books, including *Postcolonial Bergson* and *African Art as Philosophy*.